Only someone, like Marla, who knows fi[r] tree could write such an inspiring story Mango Tree Gospel gave me a voice and ...g and missions that have been stirring inside my ... ..y years. It is an exceptional story that will encourage you a... ..make you cry and be in awe of the love that God has for all of His children… It will challenge you to rethink what "Christianity" is all about. The Mango Tree Gospel is a timely message for church leaders, as well as, anyone who wants to help the hurting but doesn't know how. This book deserves a top spot on the reading list of everyone who wants to follow Jesus in a genuine practical transforming love for the broken, hurting, and needy…

Dr. Helen Delaney
Pastor-Teacher for Liberty Church of Marietta, GA/ International Speaker/ Co-Contributor for Sisters in Faith Holy Bible

This book is a must read for anyone considering working in a third world Country. The farming approach ACE uses is a win win for the farmer, the hotel and the local economy in general.

Dr. Luther B. Hughes, Jr., PhD
Associate VP for Academic Affairs (retired) Professor & Department Head (retired) Western Kentucky University Bowling Green, Ky

By weaving together the truth of scripture, the passion of testimony, and the wisdom of experience, The Mango Tree Gospel tells the 25 year old story of American Caribbean Experience. Here at ACE, churches will find hope and inspiration for vibrant and vital mission partnerships including the irreplaceable experience of short term mission trips. Anyone who is concerned with Toxic Charity or making sure that helping does not hurt must read this book. Marla Day Fitzwater and the mission and ministry of ACE are not only gifts to the people of St. Mary's Jamaica and their ministry partners in the US, but to the Church of Jesus Christ.

Dr. Brandi Casto-Waters
Pastor, First Presbyterian Church, Greer SC

It takes someone who has been working with the people of Jamaica for over 25 years to accurately portray the complexity, challenges, beauty, and courage that make up this country. In the Mango Tree Gospel, Marla presents Christ and Christianity in a practical and real way while answering the question: "what can I do". Anyone considering spending time in a third-world country really should read this book. You will gain a real sense of the incongruous lives of the people of Jamaica, while developing a real-world view of the complex issues surrounding this country. Above all you will not be disappointed.

Dr. Marie Underwood; Ed.D., CCC/SLP
Educational Leadership & Administration,
Speech-Language Pathologist, Educator

The Mango Tree Gospel

Scan the QR code to watch this introduction video

The Mango Tree Gospel

ACE's Glocal Movement in St. Mary, Jamaica

Marla Day Fitzwater
Foreword by Laura Buffington

LIFE SENTENCE
Publishing, LLC

Visit our website: www.acexperience.org

The Mango Tree Gospel – Marla Day Fitzwater

Copyright © 2014

Printed in the United States of America

First edition published 2014

LIFE SENTENCE Publishing books are available at discounted prices for ministries and other outreach. Find out more by contacting us at info@lifesentencepublishing.com

LIFE SENTENCE Publishing and its logo are trademarks of

LIFE SENTENCE Publishing, LLC
P.O. Box 652
Abbotsford, WI 54405

Paperback ISBN: 978-1-62245-157-9

Ebook ISBN: 978-1-62245-158-6

10 9 8 7 6 5 4 3 2 1

This book is available from www.acexperience.org, www.amazon.com, Barnes & Noble, and your local Christian bookstore.

An Introduction to A.C.E.

This story is dedicated to all of our supporting churches, partners, volunteers and the ACE staff who have played a part in bringing it to life. I am grateful for everyone who has caught the vision of sustainable ministry and joined me in building something that will outlast us.

Contents

Laura's Foreword

I took my first mission trip to Jamaica as an 8th grader. It was a pretty typical mission trip experience. We mixed some cement, played with kids, hosted a Vacation Bible School. We got to experience some discomfort—sleeping on floors, eating Spam and trying to avoid cockroaches. That first trip was mostly about my own development and I knew it. I knew I needed a trip like this to see the world differently, to train my heart to serve and to have compassion. I needed to know the world was bigger than the one I lived in. I needed to learn gratitude. I remember learning about joy from the people we met on the trip. Some of the things I learned that summer stayed with me for a while. Some of them faded away as soon as the new school year started. I never thought much about the bigger picture or the people we left there.

By the time I returned to Jamaica as an adult fifteen years later, the bigger picture was the only one I could see and it didn't look good. I saw the world as a broken system that nobody could ever fix. I thought things were pretty hopeless and most mission work seemed like trying to put out a raging wildfire with a teaspoon. I wasn't sure where God was in this bigger picture. Maybe in hiding. Maybe with back turned. I could blame it on "compassion fatigue," since that's trendy to have, but I wasn't tired of caring, I just didn't feel like it.

The truth is there are a lot of days when the church itself feels like a broken system that nobody will ever fix. Why export something that's broken? I find myself in conversations nearly every day trying to defend God's dream for the capital "C" church. Sometimes these conversations are with other people—sometimes they are just with the dissonant voices in my head. Loving the church and trying to search out the kingdom of God can start to feel like two separate purposes.

But that's exactly what's happening at ACE. The church, the community of faith in St. Mary and around the world, is rising up to show people what it looks like when God rules. It's a picture of faithfulness. It's a picture of the strength and joy that come from living life outside of your own range but inside the hands of God. It's a picture of people following in the steps of Jesus. It's a picture of how building things on earth can also build things that last forever. It's a picture we all need to see.

I've been telling my skeptical friends the story of ACE. I'm proud to have spent time with Marla, Allen and the staff. I love having a story I can tell about a place where God is working and people are joining in. When I find myself defending the faith, to others and myself, I think of the way they spend their days in St. Mary. I think of how broken things don't have to stay that way. We all need more stories like this to tell and the world desperately needs more stories like this to come to life.

You may be reading this because you need to take a trip. Or because you have something to give. Or something to learn. Marla says God works through ACE to help people see true things. She says God tends to get to the core of people through this place and this work. I can tell you from my time there and my time with this story, she is telling the truth. You may want a different life by the time you're done reading. You've been warned.

Prologue

"The steadfast love of the Lord never ceases,
his mercies never come to an end; they are new
every morning; great is your faithfulness. 'The
Lord is my portion,' says my soul, 'therefore I
will hope in him.'" (Lamentations 3.22-23)

It may look like just an ordinary morning, exactly what you'd expect to see in Jamaica, with all the glory and rhythm of island life. It's a desktop screensaver come to life. The sun shines. The waves crash. The mountains stand tall. The trees bear all kinds of fruit while the flowers bear all the beauty.

Of course, you have to look closer to see past
the postcards and cruise ship posters.

If you turn around from looking out over the ocean, you see cities and villages filled with people fighting to stay alive. Maybe just fighting to stay human. Jamaica is equal parts beauty and tragedy. Vibrancy and poverty. Strength and death.

On any given morning, in this particular place, the hotel staff is diligently sweeping away the dust that comes from living by the sea. Guests are swimming in the pool to celebrate some moment away from their regular life. Fishing boats glide by looking for the day's treasure, or the day's survival. On the street corners, in the makeshift aluminum scrap houses, opening their proud roadside businesses, walking to school: People are hoping to find some piece of the next world in this one.

This is where American Caribbean Experience, or ACE, lives. It's where we work, tutor, heal, serve, worship. It's where we've been trying to cultivate deep roots and bear good fruit. As I recently learned, we're basically trying to be just like the mango trees.

Our part of the island took some hits from Hurricane Sandy in

November of 2012. One of our families lost their whole house in the storm. When we went to visit, the mother was down the street at a praise and worship service, praising God right after losing everything she had, or at least the things she could hold. Brandon, one of our workers, looked around the blank space where her home used to be and tried to give her something new to hold onto. He pointed out how many trees around them had blown over but how there were a few still standing strong—all mango trees. "You're like a mango tree— you have deep roots." It turns out mango trees send multiple roots down into the soil and can reach down as far as twenty feet below the surface. As an added bonus to the illustration, mango trees bear fruit for an incredibly long time and are vital and productive for up to 300 years. In the mango tree, this faithful woman now had a picture of her own life, one steeped in things that last, that couldn't be blown over by strong winds. And we had a picture for the work God has given us in this place, as we try to invest deeply and create things that last forever. The Mango Tree Gospel.

What we're doing can also be described in business terms as we continue to reflect the "glocalization" going on in the world. As more and more companies and non-profits try to stay connected to the global world while investing locally. It turns out we've been "on-trend" for several years but we were just trying to help people survive.

It's about certain people and certain places but it's about all of us too. How God can take broken people and places all over the world and make them whole. The story of ACE is a story of God on the move. It's a story about redemption and how God restores people and places to their first and best purposes. We think more stories like this need to be told so more stories like this can be lived.

Imagine waking up every day knowing God is going to do great and unexpected things right in front of you. Maybe even through you. That's how we wake up these days in the parish of St. Mary, Jamaica. It's how we've been waking up for 25 years. To new mercies and adventures. May ours inspire yours.

Children of St. Mary

CHAPTER 1

My Story

God doesn't call the qualified,
but qualifies the called.

We repeat some things over and over because time and again, they've proven to be true. People say, "God doesn't call the qualified but qualifies the called." I say it all the time. If God only used people with stellar credentials and portfolios, it would be hard to see who was really doing the work and where the glory belonged. Fortunately when it comes to the things that matter, very few of us are qualified anyway.

I want people to know any good they see come out of our efforts is the work of God. I know how much work God has had to do on my heart. God has had to work in and through my weaknesses. God has had to carry me a long way to get me where I am today. It's this redeeming work of God that drives the ministry of ACE.

We believe that a community battling poverty, disease, illiteracy and spiritual darkness can become a place of sustainability, health, wisdom and salvation. We believe we can play a part in helping to bring the kingdom of God to earth.

This work is slow, sometimes frenzied, often heartbreaking, always exhilarating. Over the course of any given day, I may consult with our cooks over the day's hotel menu, serve as foreman on a construction project, talk administration with education officials, hold the hand of a dying infirmary patient, counsel a teenager who is trapped in darkness, barter over fish prices with local entrepreneurs, or just listen as a little girl tells a story of fear and loss.

I only make it through days like these because of the grace of God. Because God saw me not only for who I was but for who I could be. God saw my shattered, filthy, empty life and saw the potential for something else. No matter how much I resisted, God never gave up on me. That's why ACE's story starts with mine.

Nothing will foster a sense of justice in a kid quite like sibling rivalry fueled by parental favoritism. I grew up in southern Florida as the firstborn of three girls. Like most kids, I often felt like there was a competition being played out in our family and I wasn't winning.

My father was a regular source of chaos in our family life. There is always a fine line between teasing and torture (just ask someone who is being tickled), but our family had no such line and I often felt singled out as a victim. As we were preparing to head down the driveway to church one Sunday morning, I remember my dad asking me for a kiss. Everything about the picture seems just right—a precious family going to church, showing affection. But as I moved in close, he slipped a glass snake down my dress. The perfect picture moment was ruined.

I learned early on that I would have to learn how to take care of myself. I learned there would be times I would have to hide to avoid turmoil. Years later, this all made more sense to me when I heard a doctor describing the pains of childhood. He used bigger words than mine but essentially, he said that kids who grow up in tense or frustrating environments will find ways to survive. They may turn their frustration inward and spend their life with pent up emotions or they will turn their anger outward and express it to anyone in their path. I went with the latter, getting in fights and stirring up trouble. I could go from calm to explosive in six seconds flat. When you do not feel loved, by people or by God, lies take root in your heart. You do whatever it takes to be heard. To this day, when I often find myself trying to stand up for kids who don't have a voice or outlet, I am sure part of me is standing up for my childhood self.

When I was old enough to make my way out of the house, I felt like I had to choose between either attending a hyper-conservative college like my parents wanted or marrying the first guy who could take me away. In an act of desperation and rebellion, I married a man who was as far away from my parents' ideal as I could find. He was a struggling addict from Louisiana whose addictions became my addictions. I had a respectable day job, ironically in the same travel industry my family had served for so long. But over the course of five years, I also developed an addiction to recreational drugs that occasionally caused me to lose periods of time. Most of my life was spent in a highly functional high so I was promoted at work even as my addictions grew.

Although I had grown up faithfully attending church with my family, like a lot of young people running from their past, I left the church when I left home. I still heard preaching though. It was the 1980s, the height of televangelism, and my friends and I turned the 700 Club and televised church into drinking games, taking a shot whenever one of the preachers asked for money. As you can imagine, this meant we drank a lot. But for all the noise and the scandals, and despite my own twisted life, I still heard some truth come through the TV. One day, I remember distinctly hearing through the cloud one day, "God loves you and wants you to have a good and free life." I couldn't tell you who said it exactly, or how much it would cost you to receive a blessing from the one who said it. But I can tell you that the message felt new to me. It felt different from the "Believe in God because hell is hot" message I associated with the church of my youth.

Somehow, the truth made its way into my heart. On March 21, 1984, at 26 years old, I got in my car to drive home in the middle of the night from my second shift work life ready to go home and keep the party going. I remember some faceless deejay filling the space with talk about how it was the first day of spring and how the day should make us think about the rest of our lives. And then God came into the car.

That's the only way I can explain it. I remember expecting some angelic choir to start singing from the backseat because the moment felt that holy. I pulled the car over because I couldn't see through my tears. I realized what a mess I had made of my life and cried out, repeating the only words I knew to use, quoting Pat Robertson from his televised prayers. I even name-dropped Pat as I talked to God, "Pat Robertson says you'll take me anyway I am. My life's a mess but if you'll take it, I'll give it to you."

I knew in that moment God was taking the filth of my life and giving me something new.

I knew my life would be cut in half by this moment; there were the years before and they would be very different from the years after. I was lighter; the hand of God was burning away the old, dead things of my life that weren't what they were supposed to be and taking away the veil that had been covering my eyes.

I went home feeling full of possibility. I wanted my new life to include my husband and I wanted him to know the freedom I had found. I had pictures in my head of us starting over in Florida and buying a boat and living a fuller, more beautiful life than the one we had together so far. Frankly, I was also thinking about all the residual income we would have once we weren't spending money on drugs.

I thought he would feel the same excitement but when I told him I had given my heart to God and vowed not to do drugs, he saw it only as a threat to our mutually destructive way of life. But nothing could deter me from hope in the moment. For days, I trusted that he would come around, only to find out later that his infidelity was also threatening our marriage. Eventually, our marriage ended in a heartbreaking divorce but for now, I had to face days of detox, lying in bed as the room spun around me and all my bodily systems failed me.

On the first morning I woke up with everything out of my system, I fought my way out of bed to look in the mirror. What I saw looking back was a horrible reflection. I was a mess of sickness and sadness and shame. It was the truth I had been unwilling to see for the last six years. I remember praying, "God, don't let me forget how I look right now." In many ways, this is still the version of myself I see in the mirror, remembering that my best will always be just filthy rags. It's this version of myself who understands the people we serve who are caught up in a life of escape and hopelessness. I can see the shame of poverty and have compassion on people who can't see their own way out of the mess they're in.

God's work on me was just beginning. After the failure of my marriage, I went into a deep depression. Not every conversion story is neat and clean. The truth is I had lived in the mud for so long, I was like a dirty pig who couldn't tell real skin from mud. It was going to take serious work to make me presentable for any state fair show. I realized

I didn't even know my real self because I had spent so much of my life covered in sin and grime. At the time, I also didn't know how often I would see this same story played out in other people who were covered in the sin and shame of a poverty culture and had no idea who they were for real.

For weeks, I shunned help and food. I didn't want to live. I didn't want to rebuild my whole life. I just wanted to let it go. And then once again, God showed up. Just when it seemed like things couldn't get any darker in the room I had locked myself in, a huge light made its way in. I can't describe anything physical but I knew God was near. I can't tell you any words that were spoken but I knew conversation happened. You read about moments like this happening to mystic types and faithful types. But God wasn't there because I was that holy; God was there to restore my soul. Jesus was in the room as someone who loved me and understood suffering far better than I. He was the one who wouldn't tease me, or abuse me, or leave me. He wasn't just there to heal me, but to love me without conditions. I knew everything was going to be all right.

From then on, I enrolled in a crash course on faith. I went back to church. I experienced all the beautiful and difficult things that come with living faith beside other people in a church. In one church, I was asked not to return to the "singles" Sunday school class, but to instead attend the "single again" Sunday school class. But at another church, I was welcomed and nurtured by the pastor and his wife. They opened up the word of God with me and walked me through Scripture. Every Wednesday for a year, we met for dinner and Bible study. I realized I had been hungry and thirsty for the things of God for a very long time. There's nothing quite like opening up your life to the word of God. This is why I sit and read Scripture with our interns and the young people that come through our ministry. I know the power of simply listening to Scripture and arranging your life around the authority of God. This time meant everything to me. I am absolutely convinced that if we want to be a part of the story God is telling in the world, we have to get to know the script. We have to know what God has done so far and we have to listen to what God is prescribing for our lives today.

Facing the truth of Scripture and my own heart, I knew I had issues to face and started going to counseling. The anger and temper of my youth would always be there right under the surface waiting to wreak havoc on my life or anything I ever wanted to do in the calmer, stronger name of Jesus. It had to go.

I thought I was only taking the next steps of healing but all this preparation was leading me somewhere entirely different in my life.

I was single for four years, trying to find a place in the church and trying to discern what the next steps were going to be for my life. As part of a requirement for church membership, I went on my very first mission trip to the Dominican Republic.

I'm not sure about churches requiring things to belong but I suppose if you're going to do it, it may as well be getting people to leave their comfort and serve the world. I remember telling an elder of the church that I thought I could do this fulltime. It was unexpected. Up to this point, my life didn't fit the mold of a career missionary. Fortunately, God has a long history of choosing the opposite of who people expect.

It wasn't long before I found myself selling off assets and married to a man who seemed to share my passion for overseas mission work. It seemed like I had found my place. We headed to Jamaica to start a brand new marriage and life together.

I can't say we landed here with any grand schemes. I had no idea what kind of stories I would have to tell 25 years later. In fact, I learned almost as soon as we landed not to expect the expected.

Our plan was to land on the island and spend some time training under the missionary couple already established there. But within 48 hours of our arrival in Jamaica, we were on our own. The husband, who was to show us the ropes, suffered some sort of a nervous breakdown and was flown out as a medical emergency.

On their way out, our predecessors handed us a bag filled with a few files, promised us: "This is everything you need to know." It wasn't.

Their mission was built on a fairly typical model for mainline churches at the time. A somewhat "full-time" American missionary or mission- ary couple hosts American groups for short-term trips. Teams are sent out to work on building projects or to host vacation Bible schools in the local churches. This model relied on the pastor or group leader shuttling everybody around the island in a rental bus. By the end of our first summer in Jamaica, there were 17 wrecked vehicles in my name.

(Side note: Technically, I was banned from a certain rental company for at least 22 years. I only recently learned my name was clear when I tried to rent a car during a trip to Alaska.) It's not easy to navigate the terrain in Jamaica. But as I learned through that first summer, without the help of the information in the file folder with all the answers, there were all kinds of other problems with this missionary model, aside from the epidemic of American youth ministers crashing into things.

We spent two years trying to follow the established denominational mission. Of course there's a lot to learn and figure out when you're learning a new culture, along with adjusting to a new marriage and a brand new life. I started paying attention to the dynamics between our visiting Americans and the Jamaicans we knew year-round. I started seeing patterns in the people, patterns in myself, patterns in the world.

I knew that short-term trips could have great impact on American volunteers. In fact, lots of people who end up as lifelong missionaries often have their first cross-cultural experience during one of these 10 day, rental van-crashing trips. I often saw these short-term trips change the hearts and minds of visiting students and adults.

I watched American visitors make promises about coming back or sending back help.

I watched as the Jamaicans were repeatedly disappointed when Americans wouldn't follow through. I can only imagine that their newfound understanding of how the world worked and how devastating poverty is made them a new person. But they didn't know how to sustain their compassion and interest once they returned to their own section of the world.

I also watched the congregations and the Jamaicans we knew respond to the news of visiting Americans. Churches that usually only had fifteen or twenty people attend would see a giant surge in attendance when the Americans were in town. Not only would more people attend church but they would "dress down" to possibly lure the attention and sympathies of the Americans. It was a cross-cultural drama being played out in front of us every time a group would come and leave.

The Americans wanted to fix the problems of poverty as quickly and as painlessly as they could. The Jamaicans did desperate things to survive through poverty.

I started wondering if there was another way to be the kingdom of God. It seemed we were building things that could easily be blown away. I started asking whether we could do some things that would last longer than a Sunday morning or a two-week trip.

I also had to deal with my own role in these dramas. Watching these things play out, I tended to judge everyone involved.

I was particularly harsh towards the people who I thought were conniving or manipulating to get what they needed or wanted. I have this tendency—I may be the only one, but probably not—to judge other people. To punish them with my "judgment stick," thinking I know better and I behave better. But since my demons weren't their demons, I didn't understand their sins the same way I understood mine.

The same God who had rescued and
restored me started to convict me.

I heard God asking, "Have you ever been poor? Have you ever had to wonder how to feed children in your care?" While I have understood and have had compassion for pain, I have never known the particular pain of poverty. For many of us in the States, even those of us who are part of lower income families, there are safety nets in place. There are community resources and networks of family and friends. There are all kinds of "Step One" movements and programs for people who need new starts. But when poverty takes over an entire community, generation after generation, people only know desperation.

They don't know hope. And I became even more aware of the Jamaicans' complete and utter sense of hopelessness and helplessness. I found myself saying day after day: "Desperate people do desperate things." It was the only way I could put my judgment gavel away. I wanted to start understanding just how lost people perceived the Americans' presence as just another means to survive.

Eventually, we moved away from the connection with denominational mission work and started what is now ACE, American Caribbean Experience. We moved into Mandeville, up in the mountains of Jamaica to dig in and learn how to build something more sustainable. From the very beginning, part of our hope was also to partner across denominational lines. We wanted to serve and be served by churches that shared the same heart for building things that last in Jamaica.

Like a lot of mission organizations that are trying to operate in the middle of poverty, we wanted to help people with their basic needs. We hoped to follow in the way of Jesus and his disciples as they traveled among the people healing, teaching and helping them to find purpose. To keep people alive and healthy. To help them read so they could work and know the eternal words and truth of the Bible. Somehow, we wanted to help them create work so they could see the way out of desperation.

Our hope all along has been to provide real tangible hope for individuals but also to play a part in the systems we saw at work on the island. We thought we could bring in help from the U.S. in a way that had more lasting impact on both the Americans and the Jamaicans. We wanted to build relationships that lasted, to dig in relationally and get to know our neighbors. And when we did, we found difficult stories. There were people dying from toothaches and all kinds of other treatable conditions. This was shocking to me. I couldn't believe just how little access people had to such simple things. I started realizing just how much the education system in Jamaica was still under the influence of colonial thinking. I also saw just how much patience and wisdom it was going to take to build real relationships with people who saw us as "outsiders" and a means to an end.

These are the hopes that drove us in the early days of ACE. In many ways, these hopes are still driving us today. We now serve the community through education, enterprise, healthcare and discipleship. But the road from hoping to living has been a long one. And like many roads around here, it's been full of twists and barriers, and even the occasional hostage situation.

We were taking a group of visitors to enjoy some of Jamaica's natural waterfalls in the middle of the island and we had to take a wild route off the main roads (a good metaphor for most of our ministry). As we made our way, a couple of men jumped out from behind a stand of trees, ambushed our car and started helping themselves to our valuables. As if their guns weren't enough, they were also wielding giant machetes, which are fairly common on the island and take a little getting used to when you visit. They're also a little intimidating when they're inches away from major veins in your arm and are being used to cut off your watch. At one point in the mayhem, my husband had a gun to his head. I remember rolling through my mental rolodex of self-defense skills and trying to figure out if I had enough ninja moves to take these guys out. Fortunately, before I showed off my inner amateur ninja, a taxicab from nowhere carrying tourists came barreling down the middle of this wild, off-road route. Our robbers, thinking the taxi was actually a police cruiser, took off, leaving us alive but with less jewelry, less money, and less a sense of security. We filed a police report thinking it would probably be a lost cause but ten days later the police showed up with good (maybe bad?) news: The police caught our robbers but a gunfight broke out and the robbers were all killed. The police insisted that our marauders shot first and they needed me to identify the bodies before we could claim our stolen goods.

This isn't our only dangerous story. There have been other times we were threatened or found ourselves in the middle of conflict. Despite the danger, I am convinced that God watches out for those who are doing God's work. Part of an "anointing" for ministry means God covers you as you fight the battles that matter. Of course, when it comes to our time on earth, none of us are getting out of here alive so we might as well make our lives full until then. I keep the words of 2 Timothy 1.7 close to my heart (Even closer than my ninja rolodex).

I see this power at work every day, protecting our ministry and propelling us forward.

There have been other kinds of casualties along the way, including the marriage that brought me to the island in the first place. It's not easy to make a home in another culture, especially one that's devastated by poverty. While I was falling in love with the place, he was trying to run from it. He was used to fast-paced, high-pressure environments. He was a marathon runner and a driven business executive. At the time, we were living without cell phones, or internet, or any way to connect to more familiar worlds. While he struggled, I was in denial. I loved the work too much and didn't want to lose it. Eventually, I had to choose between trying to save our marriage or continuing the work.

> "For God did not give us a spirit of cowardice, but rather a spirit of power and of love and of self-discipline."

We returned to the U.S. briefly, leaving our work in the hands of some trusted partners, but it was too late. By then, we wanted different lives and he eventually wanted a different wife.

I tried to redeem the time in the U.S. by continuing my work in the travel industry. I booked trips for churches and tried to save them money so they could travel and serve. It was a way to make a living but my travel industry career also eventually served as a great cover for my true purposes in Jamaica. But for the most part, this was a situation and a season that I could not control.

While I was in Georgia, wearing the "divorced" label reminded me what it was like to live with rejection, not just from a spouse but from people who saw divorce as an unforgiveable sin that disqualified people from a faithful life. Of course, I was wearing the "twice-divorced" label which carries double the shame and burden of the "divorced" label. People could sometimes forgive or overlook one marriage failing, but two failures put me in a whole other category. People were spreading rumors and truths, both of which hurt. It made me more aware of the ways people can damage each other. On top of that, there were practical problems to consider. When I returned to Jamaica, it was also difficult to live as a single woman in a culture that is sexually charged and often treats "femininity" as synonymous with "vulnerability." I often felt the need during this season to appear tougher than I felt. Ultimately, the "divorced" label gave me a way to connect and serve people who are in pain. Jamaicans, like many of us, struggle with the power of shame and I meet a lot of people who are trying to hide parts of their lives. When it seems valuable to tell this part of my story, I tell it. It's just one more part of losing control of my own life and letting God guide me in faith.

For those who watch movies only to find out if the main character finds love or not, you should know that my story has a happy ending in that respect. After seven years of living single, I started talking to God about wanting to be married again. I was surprised by my own willingness to consider it again, much less to hear back from God that a husband might be on his way. The few stories I have about hearing words from God are strangely specific and never what I expected. That's usually how I know they are God's words and not mine. We all have a tendency to put words in God's mouth from time to time but I always trust the words that I couldn't have made up or guessed. This time, I was pretty sure I heard God say, "I will send you Allen." Usually if I think God has said something to me, I tell somebody else so they can watch for God to move with me. This time, I told a counselor. I figured the counselor would also be able to discern if I was making this stuff up. Just for good measure, I told a girlfriend too.

A few months later, I was visiting a friend in the States and decided to put in some time in a coffee shop. It was a rainy day and I was fancied up in an old sweater, even older jeans and rain-frizzed hair. I was eating a zucchini muffin, perfect for sabotaging your smile with flecks of food. But despite the potential for humiliation, I made eye contact with a guy dressed in a nice oxford button down shirt. My bravery may have been fueled by the realization that I was in possession of the only spare chair in the whole place. He sat down across the table. We started talking and didn't stop. It turned out his name was Allen. Following both God's advice, and my mother's, I took his card at the end of our conversation and invited him to church with me. It wasn't all magic— he said "no" at first because he had a full agenda that day doing manly things like cleaning his garage and watching football. Eventually he gave in. We went to church and to dinner afterwards. I told him God had told me I would marry a man with his name. Typical first date stuff. It had always been my prayer that I would eventually end up with a man who would be able to see my heart the way God does. And Allen was that man. Even my counselor thought so.

We married and he now serves with me as Executive Director of ACE and serves on our Board as well. His career also bankrolls our life and allows me to serve without financial fear. It turns out he listens to God too and feels called to support us this way. He still works in the States so we've spent more of our marriage in separate countries than we would like. As I write this, he's in the process of retirement so hopefully soon, we'll be able to live in the same place all the time. We may need to go back to the counselor when that happens so we can work through what it means to share space. We joke about this all the time but I'm pretty sure it might be for real.

Me and Allen

I tell this story partly because some people just love "love stories" and because Allen is an important part of where ACE is heading. But I also tell this story because of what I learned through this time and through meeting Allen: We can trust the good intentions of God. For a while, I thought I didn't deserve this kind of story. Sometimes other people even told me that. There were all kinds of barriers between myself and this kind of love story. But it was trust that overcame those barriers. We hear about God's love for us all the time but few of us live like that's true. I had to know God loved me before I could trust that someone else could too. When we are working through fears of failure, or the scars that come with actual failure, there's nothing more healing than hearing the assurances that can only come from the voice of God. It may be quiet and unexpected and it may offer us more than we think we can bear.

It can be a dangerous and beautiful thing to live your life dependent on the guidance and protection of God.

Of all the things we hope people see through the story of ACE, this may be the most important. We always ask God to let us live on the edge. The edge of what we think we're capable of doing. Beyond what feels safe and easy. This can be jarring to our American guests. There has been talk recently about the hostility of American culture towards faith. People get upset about Walmart greeters saying "Happy Holidays" instead of "Merry Christmas" and they cry out in the midst of this terrible persecution. Even though there may be some changes to culture, America is still a relatively safe place to follow Jesus and declare faith in God. Sometimes maybe even too safe. From where I sit on the outside, I see the dangers of complacency and comfort. If you are faithful in a safe place, you might start to get the impression that you can live life on your own. We never fall for that here in Jamaica. We know our dependence "is on God." We know that many of the things we get our hands into are outside of our control. My own prayer is always, "Let me depend on God so that I don't know how it will get done."

I see a lot of people missing out on the adventure of a life lived in faith. They never step over the edge of their own control. They never get to see God move past their own abilities.

When people visit ACE for a missions experience, we ask them to live on the edge with us. We ask them to exercise their faith and do more than they think they can do. They may end up getting worn out by a day spent playing with kids. Or emotionally drained from visiting the local infirmary. They may see things that challenge every assumption they have of how the world works. Time with us often has a way of breaking through people's hearts and tearing down their defenses. Of course, in exchange for letting us rip apart their soul for a few days, we feed them well and let them swim in the pool for an afternoon. It's a pretty brilliant exchange. It turns out Americans will try almost anything if they think they might also be able to get a tan.

Over the course of a summer full of visiting students, I'm asked the same question over and over: "Did you always see God doing stuff like this in your life?" I try to help them see that what God is doing here at ACE isn't an exception to any rule—or at least, it shouldn't be. Our story is extraordinary but it's not because God likes us better. It's just because we let God move a little more. I want every day to surprise and shock me. I don't want to settle for comfort and routine. Honestly, if I felt like some of our guests, who don't believe God is moving in their world, I'd be ready to go ahead and move on to the next stage of my life.

Sometimes these faith adventures play out over several years. There are parts of ACE's story that took years to develop. God showed me the way something could be and then five years later, it became a reality. Sometimes God shows up right in the moment, with immediate provision.

But no matter the timeline, the storyline is always the same. First, God shows us some direction to go, some future vision. Next, we take the first step only partially knowing how it might play out. Along the way, we fight against the elements at work in our world. We wait and work, sometimes patiently, sometimes impatiently, hoping we are moving toward some great ending. By every ending, we're amazed at how we got from the first step to the last.

Part of why I love telling the story of God and ACE is so that other people can see the adventures of faith play out in their lives. I'm afraid a lot of people will wake up one day and realize life has passed them by. I'm also afraid they might not.

In *The Screwtape Letters*, C.S. Lewis' great imagining of letters from one devil to another, one of the devils is advising the other on the evil power of apathy:

"You no longer need a good book, which he really likes, to keep him from his prayers or his work or his sleep; a column of advertisements in yesterday's paper will do. You can make him waste his time not only in conversations with people whom he likes, but in conversations with those he cares nothing about on subjects that bore him….so that at last he may say 'I now see that I spent most of my life doing neither what I ought nor what I liked.'.... The safest road to Hell is the gradual one—the gentle slope, soft underfoot, without sudden turnings, without milestones, without signposts."

Trade the references to books and newspapers to Netflix and iPhone apps and you'll get the idea. There's no reason why half the world should be dying and the other half should be bored to death.

ACE's story starts with mine but I'm hoping it goes much farther. I'm hoping that ACE will serve as a catalyst for generations of people to live the adventure of faith. In all kinds of ways, the world is primed waiting for people of faith to lose control of their own lives for the sake of others. The world needs Christians who can creatively engage the systems that are in place and find ways to bring them into the kingdom of God, under the rule of God. God can't wait to redeem school systems, medical care, businesses, neighborhoods, churches, villages, cities and hearts. This is the story of how ACE joined God in that work, broken lives and all.

CHAPTER 2

On Cultural Assimilation

Lessons on Cross-Cultural
Ministry that Lasts

1. Always love change. Be ready for anything to happen at any time. At the very least, this will keep you young in all the ways that really matter.

2. Create home wherever you go. Listen to your favorite music. Wear your favorite clothes. Read your favorite books. Keep some of your own culture close by.

Volunteer helping in the book club

3. Color matters. Race matters. You may always be treated as a foreigner but you could also end up being treated as a beloved foreigner.

4. Buy a lot of extra-large luggage bags for carrying ministry resources through international customs checks. Our ministry has largely been built on tools carried next to peoples' t-shirts and underwear.

5. Never mistake poverty for stupidity. Chances are the people you're serving have to make something out of nothing every day of their lives. You've probably never had to do that.

6. Never expect people to change their essential nature. Always expect God to redeem their essential nature.

7. Be yourself. Use your own words. Be careful your use of local language and culture doesn't mock the people you are trying to love. Thoughtful people in all cultures look for the deep stuff, not the superficial.

8. Be ready to accept help even more than you offer help. You probably need it just as much, if not more, than anybody else. Expect your pride to reduce in size regularly.

9. Tell your difficult stories and try not to keep secrets. Particularly in cultures dominated by shame, people need to hear truth and need to hear they are not alone. Be prepared to live in a figurative glass house—it's brighter that way.

10. Give away leadership as often as possible and with as much wisdom as possible. Don't be territorial with what God has given you. Chances are pretty good you didn't think of it yourself anyway.

Style Tips

In the early days of ACE, we encouraged our leaders and volunteers to follow the advice of all the missionaries who had been doing this before us. There was a long tradition of dressing everyday like the

Jamaicans dress on Sundays. This translated into teenage girls mixing cement in long dresses and skirts. Logistically, this seemed silly. As a fashion statement, it was messy at best. But we thought we were practicing cultural sensitivity. In reality, I eventually figured out that even as we tried to model Jesus, we were only modeling "religion." By dressing in suits and dresses, we were identifying ourselves with the traditional and legalistic version of Christianity that had a tremendous stronghold on the culture. By standing with them, we were creating a distance between our ministry and the people who had been hurt or isolated by these kinds of churches. When we would host a community event or a children's' event, we would only draw the people who were already connected to a local church and who had deemed us conservative enough for their tastes.

We already had to work at transcending racial and cultural barriers but now we were adding spiritual barriers to the mix. Our clothes were sending the message to the neighborhood that we were superior to them and could have nothing to do with them until they dressed and lived just like us.

At the risk of angering a few church boards, we changed our dress codes. If you were a visiting American, we invited you to dress like a visiting American. If you were mixing cement on a 95-degree day, you should dress for it. For some reason, this caused problems for some of our denominational supporters who started writing memos about our misdeeds. That's when I knew it was the right move. I just kept thinking about that great memo the Apostle Paul sent to the church at Galatia reminding them that the Spirit saves and not the law. How Christ came to bring freedom and to restore us to ourselves rather than to a cultural norm.

While we no longer try to imitate Jamaican styles, we do practice sensitivity by simplicity. Many of the people we serve only have a few outfits to their name. Those fortunate enough to find work often have to wear uniforms as a part of their job. For these reasons, our ACE staff wears very simple uniform shirts everyday as a way of standing in solidarity with those we serve. We also practice the "no bling" rule.

Flaunting jewelry and designer clothes sends all kinds of messages we never want to send.

In the name of simplicity, we also find ourselves teaching sensitivity when it comes to the use of electronics. You would be surprised how many people think nothing of using their smart phones and iPads in front of people who will likely never have the luxury. We've had our efforts derailed a few times because someone just couldn't wait to post on Facebook that they were serving the poor.

We've taken to limiting the use of electronics and internet access for many of our trips lately. Partly because it can harm our relationships with locals but also because we see so many Americans who are addicted to their phones and computers and can't engage in the world in front of them. We know it's a connected world and people sometimes have pressures at home to manage but over and over again, we see people using these devices to avoid challenge and ironically, connection.

Ultimately, we are trying to represent the presence of Christ in the world. In order to do that well, we find we must actually be engaged, aware and present. It's about so much more than the way we dress or the toys we use, but they are a surprisingly effective place to start.

CHAPTER 3

Enterprise

Jamaica is a noisy place. If you were reading this in St. Mary, it would come with a soundtrack of steady reggae music, and constantly beeping car horns. Somewhere in the mix, the ocean would be crashing against the shore but that noise is hardly a match for the likes of Bob Marley. It gets to be a comfort after a while, part of the atmosphere. But even more than other substances that might be associated with our island, music is a narcotic. As long as there's a loud beat somewhere, the pain is gone.

I'm sure Jamaicans love music for lots of the same reasons people all over the world love music, but at least part of the reason Jamaica loves noise is because it covers the desperation. When there are no resources, no jobs, no perceivable way out, people use whatever they can to survive. The electronic soundtrack of the island drowns out the social noise people are trying not to hear. The truth is, like many under-resourced communities, our community struggles with violence, shame and despair. There are high suicide rates. There's sexual abuse, within families, against children, often for exploitation. Once people are caught in these cycles, they feel a loss of dignity and identity. Poverty often makes people less than what God wants them to be. The Jamaicans are beautiful, resilient, joyful people but life doesn't always allow them to be their true selves. For us to care for their souls, we have had to think creatively about ways to address the systemic problems of poverty.

We've tried to find ways to give people the kind of purpose and pride that comes from working, producing, creating. For ACE, that has meant the development of micro-businesses and finding creative ways to stream money into the community and ultimately into people's families.

At least part of why I'm telling our story is because there are some things we think we've done right. There are some things that might be useful for other people trying to build sustainable ministries in poverty-stricken regions. There may even be some parts of our story that can challenge and inform churches who are looking to improve their missions model. But I feel compelled to confess that anything we do right is probably because we did it wrong the first time. The beauty of celebrating a quarter-century of missions work is looking back and seeing how far you've come.

In our early years, we didn't quite understand how to give things away to people living in poverty. It always sounds easy enough—collect stuff from people who want to give and give stuff to people who need it. But when a culture is afflicted with generational poverty, giving stuff away can hurt more than it helps.

We learned this the hard way. We once received a huge donation from an American group that sent giant containers of clothes and goods to non-profits. In our naiveté, we thought we could just give the stuff away. Within fifteen to twenty minutes of setting up shop, we had a crowd of 300 people literally fighting each other for free stuff. We learned that we could not act like Santa Claus; it led to a violent Christmas, even more than some of our family fights around the tree. We couldn't sweep in and shower people with gifts if we wanted to make changes that would last.

> After our first failures, we decided
> to set up a different kind of shop.

We decided to try setting up makeshift thrift stores with the donations we received. We took over a school or an empty space for a day and sold the goods for a very minimal price. You would be surprised how charging just a few cents for a t-shirt slows down the fight. We then put any and all profits back into the community—usually to schools we supported. We have learned that we need to keep money flowing through the community and also to help people understand value. We think we may have learned to give in a way that helps the system instead of upsetting it.

When ACE first landed down from the Jamaican mountains and in the parish of St. Mary, I was the only white woman in town. I understood by then, even if I lived permanently in Jamaica, I would always be an outsider. The roots and damages of colonialism run deep in Jamaica. For much of their history, Jamaicans were forced to take on other people's lives—they had to take on their dress, their language, their ways of life. I learned early on from a retired school teacher-turned-missionary that Jamaicans preferred for some things to be their own. As we shopped in the market one day, I used "Patois," the Jamaican dialect that's part-Creole, Africa and broken English. As a mentor, she corrected me, "They don't like you to pretend that you're them." It was an infringement, a violation, for me to take on their language. Even if I understand their language, I learned to answer in my own. To respect their boundaries as the outsider that I am and will always be. They respected me and I was building trust in the community but I wanted to invest in the community in a more permanent, tangible way. We needed "brick and mortar"—we needed to make a home in St. Mary and find a way to affect the local economy.

It had been a dream of mine for a while to buy a hotel—maybe one that had passed its prime and redeem it. I thought we could do the work of God by restoring the hotel to its' earlier glory and to a new purpose. We could provide this community with a safe, attractive hotel for Jamaicans and tourists alike. We could use it as a micro-business, to make some money and put it back out into the community through schools, health clinics and small business loans. We could put down roots. We could create something that would last and even keep itself going. I was dreaming Mango.

We also needed some place to put our visiting American teams. In the beginning, when teams came to serve out in the community, we housed them in an old crowded hotel filled with bunk beds. Of course, we could have just pitched it as part of the full experience, to live in rough conditions and to grow spiritually through perseverance. But it actually started getting dangerous. We had students getting shocked by faulty wiring. Our septic line was always backing up. We actually drew the attention of Jamaica's Ministry of Health who didn't want visitors staying in these facilities.

I remember being angry with God, thinking God's provision had somehow failed us. Here we were trying to affect lasting change for

God's kingdom but we were growing faster than God had expected or planned for, apparently. I remember telling God off, falling into that trap of thinking I knew more and could see more than God could. We all get riled up at God at times and feel like we have to get loud about it. So I did. I went out on the balcony of the crumbling hotel, worried that I might fall through the floor and pointed my complaints in the direction of that night's harvest moon.

Usually when you yell at God, you don't expect an answer. As much as we say we want answers, it's not exactly a moment we want God to catch us in. But this time, God got loud right back.

Right there in the middle of my rant, I heard as clear as could be, "I will give you Tradewinds." You could accuse me of making this up if you want, but I didn't know what "Tradewinds" was. It's not like one of those prayers where I made God say what I wanted. I didn't know what God was talking about.

Until the next day. When the owner of an old hotel down the road called "Tradewinds" stopped by because he'd heard I was interested in a hotel. You would think I would have immediately seen this guy as an answer to prayer. But since he was a stranger and he was asking me to go look at his hotel, I was instead sizing him up and making sure I could take him if necessary.

It turns out he had grown up in the area but had moved on. The hotel had been intended as a gift for his daughter but there were not enough tourists in the area to keep the business going. Plus, as daughters will do, his had fallen in love and decided to move away. He was desperate to sell and I think he hoped I would lease it, improve it and then give it back for him to make a profit.

Still, I knew it could be God moving, but there were obstacles. Money, for instance, which we didn't have. I decided to go look at the property anyway. It turns out I had been driving right by it for years. From the road, all you could see was tiny security hut with a single light bulb inside hanging over the head of the elderly watchman.

The place had been vacant for years. The pool was filled with water that could easily pass as black coffee. The rooms were occupied by mold. The toilets didn't work and neither did the air conditioning. The grounds were all wild and overgrown.

But that's not what I saw. Somehow, my eyes were open and when I looked at the Tradewinds, I saw what it could be. Maybe like God saw me that morning when I woke up ready to be done with the old and onto the new. I saw something finished even though there was only a mess.

I knew this could and should be the home of ACE. It was God's leading. But also, God would have to negotiate this business deal.

The owner proposed a deal to us. My attorney said it was an awful one. I had to choose between listening to the attorney and listening to God. I know the right answer might seem obvious. I went with the attorney. Something wasn't right. I could only keep wrestling and waiting.

A couple years later, after the owner kept trying to offer the hotel to people, a hurricane changed the game. In 2004, Hurricane Ivan came along and took the roof off the primary school just down the street from the hotel. It turns out the owner had a connection to that school and when I called to see if he wanted to help ACE rebuild the school, he agreed. His heart seemed to be softening. In truth, I believe God was working on him through our whole relationship.

I decided it was time for some counterintuitive business decisions. As we worked together on the school project, I asked the owner if we could help him sell his hotel. I asked if we could rent the hotel for just a week and send in a team to clean it up for potential buyers. In essence, we paid to rent the place and clean it for him. The offer was sincere. And yes, a little foolish.

ACE sent a pioneering group of American teenagers to camp out on the grounds of the hotel since the insides weren't fit to live in. They cleaned and painted and cleaned and painted some more. By the end of the week, when he saw the work these kids had done, and when we handed him a check for the week, his heart was broken. We cut a deal.

God and the landlord gave us the property on a three-year lease with an option to buy. Over the next few years, we put money into the worn-out old "Tradewinds" and turned it into the fresh and clean "Galina Breeze," hoping the name might match a new wind moving through the Galina community. Halfway through the lease, long before the place officially belonged to us, and against Allen's sensible concern, I sealed the name on the bottom of the hotel pool as an act of faith that the promise of God would come true in time. I was also sealing in people's perception of me as, well, nuts.

Whenever visiting churches would ask whether ACE owned the property, I would explain that we owned it in the supernatural world, but not the natural...yet. I always knew that when it came down to paying the bills, I had a connection to a God who had a thousand cattle on a thousand hills, which is just the Bible's way of letting us know God has already done the math. Eventually, through the movement of God, members from one of these churches helped us to make the down payment on the hotel and buy our ministry's home base. God's words spoken to me in the middle of my anger were coming true. Basically, their money was shutting me up. Even though the selling price now was less than what the owner first offered, we still couldn't quite make it. Donations and offerings were coming in from all kinds of places but 30 days before closing, we still found ourselves $28,000 short. I remember telling God, "You didn't bring us to the dance floor to not provide the music."

I wrote 30 letters asking for $1,000 from people who I thought were most likely to give. I ended up with $35,000 from just seventeen of the people. We had our brick and mortar. And our swimming pool and ocean view.

People in mission work get to see God work this way all the time.

Original hotel after a white wash paint job. (2005) No hot water and no a/c

Galina Breeze 2013

Where churches and organizations can sometimes fear cost and money issues, it's actually a great opportunity to learn to trust and lean on the faithfulness of God. We never tell sad stories about money at ACE. We've seen too much provision to ever wonder where our resources are going to come from. We have also seen how often God works on the hearts of the people who give. I always wonder about the people who hold on so tightly to their money and their fear. They never get to see God do great and real things in the economy of the Kingdom.

Even now, as the hotel is fully ours and fully functioning, there are seasons when we're not completely sure how all the bills will get paid.

There are days we have had to ask God to send us business. Our Jamaican hotel staff often joins us in these prayers—sometimes they even start them. Our hotel manager, Althia, who oversees the bookings, saw a gap in a season and knew things were going to get tight. She knew the answer was to pray. Within days, we had booked exactly the number of events and guests we needed to make it through the month.

The beautiful thing about the provision of God through the hotel is that we are able to invest money and gifts right back into the community. We provide jobs to Jamaicans who know the hospitality industry and do it well. We even offer them with benefits and health care where other well-known resorts often do not. We try to treat our staff with respect and love so they can know their real value is so much more than a paycheck. We can buy local foods from the farmers to serve our guests delicious, authentic cuisine. We can invite the local organizations to use our pool and our property for their celebrations and their life events. Also, we can send our profits back out into the community to finance local trades and crafts.

As poverty continually threatens the community, we are always looking for ways to simultaneously put money back into the economy and helping people to see their true worth. We want people to know that God made them to produce, to create, to work and to live life abundantly. We want people to know that God can provide for them in ways that their economic and political system may not.

We have tried to shift from offering people short-term help to training them for long-term life economic stability. This is why we support the development of businesses over building homes. This can be hard for visiting Americans to understand, especially if they are used to other short-term experiences that are largely based around building projects. When you're faced with a community of 500 people who need homes, it gets messy to just start building. New homes create isolation and conflict in our communities. Occasionally, through humanitarian groups or church groups, someone will acquire a brand new home. We have seen this go very badly. Land ownership also works differently here. Too often, the corruption of the system will wipe away good intentions. ACE learned this the hard way. We once helped an abused woman build her own home on land she thought was hers to develop. We built her a typical two-bedroom block house so she could live on her own and live safely and comfortably. Within a month, the "owner" of the property, who may have really owned it or may have been exploiting her, reclaimed the land and took over the home as his own. It may have been that she didn't understand the difference between leasing and owning land, but we also failed to investigate the situation. We didn't want to make this mistake again. When we do engage in building projects, it's usually with the families connected through our child sponsorship program and often on already existing homes. We try to use the projects as an opportunity to teach. When poverty takes over in a person's life, they sometimes make foolish choices while looking for simple and easy solutions. We've had people trade in homes for places they couldn't really afford. We've seen people try to use the system and its' brokenness to their benefit. We've also had people try to get out of us whatever they could without investing anything themselves. If we build or invest, we are always looking for people who will join us in the work. This may mean they provide building supplies. It may mean they help us with the construction. It always means that they show signs of wanting a different life for their sake and for their family.

Volunteers constructing a bathroom and kitchen for a single mother

Just as Galina Breeze fuels our ministry and our community involvement, we support other micro-businesses as a way of investing in people's lives and well-being. There are a lot of Christ-centered efforts to resource people in developing countries through building sustainable businesses. We probably share some things in common with some of those groups but we probably do some things differently too.

Moving money around in a poverty-stricken community is certainly a complicated thing. There are days when our role feels more like "loan sharking" than Christian ministry. We tend towards demanding high accountability from the people we support. We find it to be motivating and hope it's motivating enough to help people break generations of poverty cycles.

In a place where people are desperately trying to survive, we get many requests for loans to start businesses, or just loans to get by. I imagine Americans understand this desperation in a different way today than they might have ten years ago when loans were handed out like toothbrushes at the dentist. With all the needs and the requests, we've had to find ways to discern where and when and with whom to invest.

Again, lots of the things we do now come from doing them the wrong way first. Today, we try to spend time with people through the process. We interview them and ask them some questions about their relational health and their religious affiliations (most people here have them whether or not they live them).We look for ways to mentor and guide people through the process of starting and sustaining a business.

We found Vinn the tailor the same way a lot of people find artists and craftsmen they trust—through word of mouth. We wanted to buy school uniforms for several children at the school and started wondering if they could be made locally instead of the traditional "Made in China" attire. We do everything we can to eat and spend locally. We heard that the father of one of our hotel employees was a tailor. Sure enough, when we arrived at Vinn's house in the mountains to request twenty school uniforms, he was sitting at an antique sewing machine, smoking a joint the size of a toilet paper roll. Vinn is a Rastafarian who loves talking about his religion. The marijuana is part of his spiritual routine but we found we had other things in common with Vinn. Like most Rastas, he loves growing natural things and ACE was working just down the street to help his neighbor with a farming project. You can tell Vinn is trying to find holiness. He has reverence for people and for the natural world. We've never asked him to give up his religion to work with us. His faith is his identity and would mean major change for his life and self-understanding. But he often puts the joint out to talk with me and calls me "Sister Marla" as a sign of respect. We sometimes have conversations about Jesus and we treat each other with mutual kindness and appreciation. After a few years, Vinn has made over 300 uniforms for the kids in our schools and we've paid him for his fine work. The Jamaican press just did a story on Vinn and his thriving business. He credits "Jah" with helping him make a living but someday Vinn may see that his life and work are a credit to Jesus.

Vinn working his machine

Down the street from Vinn is our business partner, Lorna. She's a single mom of three kids who lives in a board house without plumbing. She's sent one of her children off to college already. She farms her land without any of the equipment that might be standard for a farm in other countries. She spends fifteen hours a day out in the heat with only her hands, a hoe and a machete. When she asked for a loan to build a chicken coop and raise some chickens, ACE helped her to write a business plan so her profits might multiply. She received her loan from ACE supporters and used the profits to grow new crops and buy more chickens. Today, ACE is able to use her farm to test out new farming experiments and she's working part-time with our housekeeping staff at Galina Breeze.

We have supported the local snack industry by supporting our friend, Ramone. Ramone bakes bulla, a sweet ginger bread, and jackass corn, a peanut brittle concoction without any peanuts. He sells his goods to local grocery stores. What used to be a small home business has grown to needing extra space. With growth, he's also needed to meet health codes and hire help. Ramone has more demand than he can keep up with and keeps bringing people along with him as he tries to supply his world with good treats. Through our Green Life Farm projects, ACE has been able to restore natural instincts and resources for farming in the community. We've built several partnerships with local farmers and loaned them the money and materials to build slow-drip irrigation systems on their property. When necessary, we've also supplied them with organic seeds provided through donations or through greenhouses we've built. Since security is also an issue for farmers, we've helped them to build fences guarding their harvest. We also figured out we could grow things that people didn't necessarily recognize as valuable crops and hide them right out in the open. We help our farmers think through growing the kinds of crops that the restaurants in Ocho Rios or other area resorts might need. Since some of our farmers lack trucks or transportation, we also help them get their harvest to people who will buy it. Sometimes we are the buyers—our hotel is filled with locally grown food that is almost always attached to a story about transforming a person's life. While we walk our farmers through as much of the process as we can, they are building the business muscles they need to keep their farms growing.

As the local food movement continues to catch on in America as a way to show the world you are "on-trend," it's a way of survival here. Not just for eating fashionable food but for building a sustainable life.

On one level, our involvement in microbusinesses has to do with survival, keeping families alive and financially viable. But on a whole other level, we are trying to teach and show the economy of the kingdom of God, where nothing is wasted and where the right investments last forever.

An abandoned hotel becomes a hub for the work of God. The vacant lot brings a harvest of delicious food. The hands that may have once been idle now make beautiful things. It's never "just business" when God is on the move.

CHAPTER 4

On Money

MacGyver, local farmer, with his water tank that he received a micro-business loan of $1500 to keep his crops alive during the drought

We invest in small businesses and the local economy of St. Mary because there are countless connections between financial health and spiritual health. This is just as true in your community as it is in ours. Finances are linked to the heart, whether it's a place that doesn't have enough or a place with more than enough. As the leader of an organization that serves as a channel for resources to move from one place to another, I get to see the effects of giving on both the receivers and givers and here are some things I've learned:

While God calls us to be generous, God also calls us to be smart. I have seen people go bankrupt in order to fund ministry. God seems to be about the "long game" in all kinds of ways. Making short-term decisions at the expense of your long-term future seems counter to God's ways. Giving is absolutely essential. Smart giving may be even more essential.

If God calls you to do something with your life in the world (and if we're listening, we're always called....to something), then you should be the first one willing to make a financial investment. Find creative ways to contribute to the work you're doing. Use your skills to keep income actually coming in. Give a portion, maybe a tithe, to your own work or your own organization. For 21 years, my income came from work outside of ACE. I know this can't always be the case for people, but I believe the principle is still true: if you find ways to invest financially in your own non-profit or ministry work, you will love the work in a different way. If Jesus is right (and he usually is) and our hearts follow our treasures, make sure yours are in the right place.

If you are trying to raise financial support, consider it a great privilege to talk about what you're doing and what God is doing through you. Get excited about the risk of relying on God and provision. Don't let pride keep you out of life's greatest game. I see people who are too afraid to ask for resources so they end up missing out on giant possible adventures. Trust that God will show up strong in the search for money and resources.

As you tell people what God's up to, encourage them to join in and avoid the temptation to appeal to their selfish interests. Don't promise to put their name on bricks and benches (though you may want to be open to the possibility if it means that much). Remind them of the eternal significance of giving instead of the temporal. It's not about getting recognition and having everyone know what they've given. Help them to see that there is a much bigger story being told than tax breaks and incentives. God is working in powerful ways and they get to be a part. Help them to see giving as a spiritual exercise, one in which they will get to see God show up faithful in their lives every day.

Make it a lifelong habit to sow into the lives of people you meet. Test out the promises of Scripture that tell us we will reap what we sow. Live your life in such a way that you are constantly pouring into other people without any self-interests. Don't look for immediate results. Just love and listen. Even if you start off doing this so it will pay off, eventually, you will have acted selflessly enough that it will become who you are and not just something you're trying out.

When possible, give anonymously. Years ago, when I was making more money than I needed through commission sales, I heard about a pastor of mine who needed money. He and his wife were planning a trip to Ireland to make a life-long dream come true. He had left his wallet with all his money for the trip at the bank and by the time the wallet made it back to him, the money was gone. When I found out they were going to have to cancel their trip, I told my boss I was going to provide them the money. My boss wisely advised me to give anonymously. This was not my plan but I tried it anyway. It wasn't easy. Part of me wanted them to know. Years later, my pride was tested even further when I ran into the couple and they recounted the story or receiving the anonymous gift. They called it "one of the most unbelievable faith things" in their life. As they told the story, they said they suspected who gave them the money. I leaned in, expecting my generous deed to pay off in a grand gesture of gratitude. But they thought it was someone else. And my secret was still safe and my pride still had a long way to go. I may have just undone any work God was doing in me by keeping that secret, but trust me, giving without immediate reward is good for the soul.

If you are looking to give to a non-profit organization or ministry, as an individual or as part of a church or other group, reward financial responsibility. Look for organizations who practice good stewardship. Look for clean financial slates. We spend a lot of time and resources at ACE to keep good reports and to stay out of debt. Strangely enough, our financial responsibility sometimes turns givers away. I've seen a number of occasions where church boards were trying to decide where to send financial support and opted to send their money to groups who were in dire straits because of poor money management. Financial supporters like being able to answer emergency calls and feel like they are making a bigger impact by giving to the organization that "needs it more." We have made it a policy at ACE, even when our budget is strained, to avoid the appearance of desperation. We avoid it partly because we are careful with what we have, but also because we trust God to provide.

We try to avoid worrying over money and to see it instead as a way to constantly see the provision of a God who knows our needs before we do.

When you invest in a missions organization, either financially, or with your time, or your prayers, remember the kind of stress that comes with living and working in a different culture. Be careful to apply things you think you know to their contexts. We often get advice from well-intentioned guests who see only a little bit of what we do but think they know how we can do it better. We know we have things to learn but trying to move work forward in another culture is a complicated business and those of us who spend our lives on the field greatly need your support and understanding.

CHAPTER 5

Education

The story of our involvement with Jamaican students and the future of the island starts with laying the past to rest.

In my earliest days of ministry, I lived in a very rural area of the island and I played whatever role I could to get to know people and to help them know and trust me. This included transporting the bodies of people who died to the nearest morgue. My silver pick-up truck became their long, black limousine, taking bodies from the place of their death to their celebration of life. Or at least carry them as far as the place where they would be frozen until their family could raise enough money to bury them honorably. In addition to grief, funerals can become a huge financial burden to a family who feels the social pressure to honor the dead through a giant celebration, spending money that could be invested in the future of their family instead of the past. The grieving process is complicated by poverty—they believe in holding grand funerals to say "goodbye" but they often have to wait a long time to build up the funds for the elaborate funerals. The transporting, especially back then, was complicated too. When someone died, they were wrapped in sheets and laid on two by fours for easy movement. And then they were placed in the back of my truck. As the unofficial funeral taxi, I had a hard time watching this process. It was always hard for me to accept that people who had lived full and lovely lives were now being carried around in sheets in the back of my truck. Grandmas who had rocked kids to sleep their whole lives ended up on boards and carried the same as a bale of hay. Even though they wanted to treat people with dignity, poverty often left them to crude means.

I was also the funeral musical director. I went from driving the funeral truck to playing the piano for the service. Since they throw such elaborate funerals, I often found myself playing for three or four hours. Trust me when I say, no matter what the advertisements say, no make-up can survive a Jamaican funeral. I was a cosmetic nightmare by the end of these services. As an added bonus, the bodies that had been frozen for preservation were often thawing during the services, filling the room with a difficult odor. Almost always, the lone circular fan that provided some comfort from the heat ended up blowing the fragrance of warming death right in the direction of me, the melting piano player.

Eventually these funeral jobs led to other opportunities. I became the church choir director for the Christmas program. I know it sounds a lot more glamorous than driving the "truck of death" but this job had its difficulties too.

I knew this church could sing.

I heard them singing old hymns at the top of their lungs every Sunday morning. But for some reason, the songs from the Christmas program were a real struggle. The people just could not learn the words. Then I noticed that some of their song sheets were upside down and they had no idea. They might as well have been written in Latin. It never occurred to me that the choir couldn't read. And of course, they wanted me to think they could. Shame kept their struggle a secret so we stumbled along, with me assuming they could learn the words and them not knowing which way to hold the music sheets.

It's a mistake I have not made again.

Eventually, I put all their music on tapes. (Remember tapes?) Choir members could take the music home and learn by listening. We made it through Christmas but I realized literacy on the island was a major problem and ACE needed to figure out how to help.

Even though Jamaica declared their independence from Britain in 1962, in many ways, the island is still held captive by the system that held them down for so long. It makes sense that it would take Jamaicans a while to find their way as their own people and their own place. British influence is seen in everything from their "Constabulary" police force to their affection for their game of Cricket to their government. Some of this influence is positive and provides rootedness and structure.

A typical primary school classroom

Their educational method is still strongly influenced by the colonial-slave method of teaching: the teacher recites things and the class says it back, learning by repetition and recitation. The children are meant to memorize words rather than process them. If you have a good memory and perform well, you can copy and mimic your way to the top of the class.

The whole day in a traditional Jamaican classroom is scripted. The teacher engages the class through a rehearsed conversation. They say daily prayers, they follow routine conversations before and after lunch or recess. The same words day after day. Imagine a classroom where the teacher is trying to teach the students a foreign language and the vocabulary is limited. You would only use certain familiar phrases. In fact, this is exactly the way American students often learn Spanish or French. The teacher leads the class through rehearsed dialogue: "How are you?" "I am fine." "What is your name?" "Me llamo Marla." This process may work when it comes to a second language but when you are learning your own world this way, it can be very limiting. The Jamaican educational system makes no allowances for kids who need a different way of learning and since many of these children come from low-income, high-stressed environments, it's no wonder that they make it to adulthood without knowing which way the music sheets should go.

The system also stifles creativity. There is only one way to learn, one way to succeed, one way to express yourself. But this one way isn't working for a large majority of children in the system.

When ACE decided to get involved with the local schools, we looked for schools with the lowest literacy rates. Many of them were rural schools, buried up in the mountains with little access and very few resources. We also looked for strong principals—for leaders who wanted something different for their schools and their children.

We could have started our own school. We could have replaced one colonial system for another. We decided instead to engage the community where it was and to try to infuse the system with new life. We believe this follows the model of Jesus, incarnating into the world, meeting humanity in its struggle. We also believe this could lead to changes that last longer and reach further.

ACE started building partnerships with principals and their schools. We wanted to be a resource for them without enabling them. We wanted to avoid the same mistakes of the colonial systems by helping them figure out how to be a better version of themselves, instead of being who we think they should be. Instead of saying, "We can do it and you can help," we wanted to tell principals and teachers, "You can do it and we can help."

They need to hear this. Like lots of teachers and administrators, their days are long and their obstacles many. Remember, this is a noisy culture. And the lack of resources contributes to the noise in a Jamaican school. Oftentimes, classrooms don't have real physical walls so the first grade teacher may find herself yelling over not just her own students, but the students and teacher in the "room" to her right and her left. The students often come into the room after filling up on the standard high-sugar Jamaican snacks and sweeter than sweet juice boxes. (Imagine 50 kids in a classroom on a major sugar high on a 95 degree day and you might at least understand a little of the Jamaican teachers' dilemma.)

In addition to the literal noise, there is the cultural and social noise as well. Schools often become gathering places for transient or idle folks looking for a place to sit and watch the days go by. Schoolyards become like the local city corner where people may just gather to hang out or they may show up with far more dangerous plans. Some of our schools have become targets for sexual predators looking for easy prey. We've had kids attacked in the back lots of the schools during recess or even pulled out of the classroom. It's pretty tough to teach kids the alphabet when they fear for their lives and the loss of whatever innocence they might have left. They live in a world filled with all kinds of noise. They end up living out the violence they see around them. Playful back-and-forth escalates quickly to acts of aggression and anger. Teachers spend a good portion of their day as referees trying to keep the fights fair.

Galina Primary

Lots of mission work in poverty-stricken countries focuses on children. I'm sure there are lots of good reasons for this. Children are often unwilling victims in systems of poverty. In places where people are fighting to survive, the care and nurturing of kids is often overlooked. I'm sure part of why ACE has focused so much energy on children and education has to do with my own tendency to want to protect the underdogs and the most vulnerable members of the community. I always had a heart for children, even if I was never sure I wanted to raise my own. Unlike my sisters who cared for their baby dolls and went on to have kids of their own, I never saw myself raising a child. (Strangely enough, I have actually always loved teenagers. Most people can't say that, including parents!)

We often come across children in
incredibly vulnerable situations.

Once, I was volunteering at a children's home when I heard scratching sounds coming from a closet. They sounded wild, like an animal might be trapped. When I opened the door, I found a little boy who was being treated like a wild animal with only a water bowl to keep him company in the closet. His hair and nails grew out of control. He was three feet high and about eight years old. He was small for his age and had been labeled mentally handicapped even though his only impairment was his deafness. I hugged him as soon as I saw him and he squeezed me right back. The closet couldn't take away his humanity. It only took a short while for me to find the means to send him to a deaf school, along with providing him a home when school was out. I learned over time he had been born with hearing but at some point in his short and tragic life, he had lost it. His story was too typical of the time: In the 1980s, Jamaica had one of the highest deaf populations per capita because of the lack of care for infants. But because of ACE's intervention, this story is atypical—this child is now a healthy adult with a full-time job who follows Jesus everyday of his life. He's thriving and reminds us how powerful it can be to be in one place long enough to see the whole story play out. The healing of God sometimes plays out over years but it's always beautiful to see.

ACE makes learning fun

We need these stories to give us hope when we run into vulnerable kids in the community. Even now as I write this, there are two kids just down the street from the hotel who have made a home out of a couple boxes. Not too long ago, I sat and talked with a seven year old who had never seen the ocean even though he spent his whole life within walking distance of the shore. We serve kids because we want to restore this season of their life to what it should be—a time for nurturing, learning and exploring.

But we also focus on kids because they encourage others to hope. In every face, in every classroom, we see potential—something great could come from this child's life if only we could interrupt these long-established cycles early. If only we could shower these children with affection and protect them from aggression. We could silence the noise of the world and fill this child with the good truth from God. We see what could happen if this child could maintain the playful but strong spirit God gave him or her. This child's curiosity could become a search for something great. If only this generation could see their own potential to rise up out of the patterns of destruction. Once in a while, in children, we get to see some glimpse of what Jamaica could be. We are there when children start to learn new words. We get to help the creative kids break out of the normal form and structure and color outside of the lines to make beautiful things. We get the great privilege of seeing kids move away from formal, rehearsed prayers and speak to God like God might really care about them. As the future of the country, we want to play a part in helping them to live the full lives God wants for them. We hope someday they might lead others to do the same.

We offer schools all kinds of resources. We offer tutoring, teacher mentoring, extracurricular programming, field trip assistance. Occasionally, we help with building needs or security needs. In return, we ask for their receptivity and cooperation. We often tell them, "We will give—you give back." One way we foster this cooperation is by asking the Jamaican teachers as often as possible, "How can we help?" We give them the opportunity to tell us what they need. Giving them the chance to voice their hopes and their struggles gives them ownership of their classroom and their success.

We try to give them this opportunity through genuine conversation, over lunch or through training sessions. We bring in teachers from the States to meet with them and mentor them. We sometimes supply substitute teachers so the teachers can get away to learn and grow themselves. We try to keep these relationships going over time so trust grows. Often we ask them to reflect on their own education. We help them tap into the ways they learn to read, hopefully giving them the chance to see what might be effective in their classrooms.

There are certainly days when it would be easier for us to walk in and show them just how Americans do it but this assumes that our way should be theirs and puts us once again in a dominant role, trying to make them more like us and less like themselves.

Of course, doing work this way requires working within a system that can be difficult to maneuver. Like a lot of systems in the world, the systems in Jamaica are reflections of human brokenness and limitations. We have had to learn how to operate within a system that will always treat us as outsiders. We often find ourselves mixed up in battles for power that we aren't trying to fight. Particularly when we are offering to put money or resources into a school, there are hoops we have to jump through—hoops that seem to move every time we get close. The Jamaican systems move slowly, partly for fear of failure, partly because of the ever-present messiness of bureaucracy.

Again, the effects of generations of colonialism can be seen in the way their different political ministries operate. Often decisions are made in Kingston, the capital city, by people who are removed from the situation. The local players want to look like they have control even though they are dependent on power from far away. Decisions are made slowly if at all. Even people who have risen through the ranks of society struggle with the shame of their past and their surroundings. They worry about looking foolish or being part of something that fails. They also cannot shake the habits of poverty, sometimes asking for more than we can give, or asking for something that would only solve a temporary problem instead of the lasting ones.

Trying to work alongside a system that's broken brings a lot of different tensions. On one hand, the government of Jamaica will admit that their system is outdated and needs retooling. But since they have not made any great strides to overhaul the whole system, they sometimes try to cover over the weaknesses with deception. We also have to live with the tension of knowing that Scripture calls Christians to submit to authority, but knowing that the authority around here can sometimes be prone to corruption and abuse. We have to make decisions all the time about how to operate alongside deep-seeded dysfunction. We often ask people coming on trips to bring supplies in their suitcases. Over the years, people have carried in paper products, medicines, tools, children's shoes— all tucked away in their suitcases. But if they were to claim all these items coming through customs, there's a good chance the goods would be taken, or at least used to draw out money for customs. We have to ask people to consider the greater good although it can sometimes challenge their moral compass. When you put the same questions into a more extreme context, like smuggling Bibles into China, people see the dilemma a little more clearly. It's a tension we live in but did not create.

We think Jesus may have had us in mind when he told his followers to be "wise as serpents and innocent as doves." It's not easy to adjust moral and ethical codes to apply them in another country but it's often necessary to serve. It's not an easy line to walk but we try.

We once started a simple project to repair a security wall around a school. What seemed like a simple project became a lengthy season of school board meetings, appointments with attorneys, and consultations with engineers. In the end, after lots of correspondence and political posturing, we did exactly what we set out to do. I had to surrender to the system, letting them think the solutions were all their ideas. I had to slow myself down and let the officials experience what ownership felt like, since many of the players involved often feel like puppets to the system themselves. There were certainly moments I wanted to do away with their systems completely, followed by moments of letting their systems work for me. All in the name of serving the community and making sure kids could play circle games at recess without fear of being abused.

We have also found some ways to bypass the system and invest directly into the lives of the students in our partner schools. Much of the noise and chaos in the classroom follows the kids to school from home. As we started working in the schools, we started noticing how often kids regularly missed school. Many of their attendance issues can be linked to lack of resources, with some of the kids even lacking clothes to put on in the morning. The Jamaican school system requires kids to wear uniforms, including proper shoes, to school. Kids would miss school because they were forced to share shoes with their brothers and sisters and it wasn't their day to have shoes. They would miss because they were hungry. Sometimes they had to miss a day because there was no underwear—when you've always had this in your life, you don't realize that it's actually a luxury! Kids would miss because they couldn't pay school fees. Sometimes their parents were just so busy trying to survive, they didn't have the energy or motivation to make sure the kids made it to school.

The three musketeers happy to have a safe haven at school provided by ACE

We answered the problems of poverty with a system of our own. We started asking our guests and our ministry connections to sponsor the kids we knew were missing school for preventable reasons. We helped families to pay for school uniforms, school supplies, good shoes, lunches, transportation and Christmas and birthday presents. (This may seem superfluous to some of you but it wouldn't if you had never had them.)

As a part of ACE's child sponsorship program, we regularly visit the homes of the children we're supporting. This gives us an entryway into their lives and helps us to build relationships with the entire family. We're able to start conversations with family members about how they're making ends meet and how they're caring for the children. It also just gives us a chance to practice the ministry of listening. Our visits give people a place to talk about how things are hard. If they want, they can tell us life is difficult or tell us what creative and brave things they're doing to get by.

Just getting to our students' homes is sometimes a treacherous affair. Jamaican homes are often built into the sides of mountains or in the depths of valleys. The roads are all less-traveled here. The homes themselves are often one-room buildings fashioned out of scraps of aluminum panels or whatever building materials they could scrape together. The floors are often pieced together from cardboard. Often several homes share an outdoor kitchen or bathroom. In the slums closer to the city, the bathroom waters flow through the neighborhood in makeshift tunnels that go along the sidewalk. Even homes without working lights will have working televisions and VCRs—essential for drowning out reality and helping people to live somewhere else in their minds for a while.

Visiting students' homes gives us a chance to ask what else we might be able to do. Occasionally, we're able to help people with building projects. We may be able to build them a working latrine.

Sometimes these home visits lead to creative repurposing. Lately we've been supplying people with lights: it turns out that rum bottles filled with chlorine can light a home for months. Just further proof that nothing in the kingdom of God goes to waste.

When we visit homes, we always ask where the children sleep. Oftentimes, they don't have a designated bed for the child. If they do, sometimes it's a makeshift situation with mattresses and pillows that are nothing but casings stuffed with newspapers. We had a high school student from the states who was looking for a project. We needed mattresses. We also knew the people at the infirmary nearby needed new mattresses as well since many of their beds were twenty years old and covered in the kinds of stains that come with nursing home life. This student secured the money for 20 brand new mattresses, wrapped in

Volunteer installing a rum light

1 cap of chlorine + 1 bottle of water = 1 rum light good for 6 months

vinyl and delivered to us fresh from Kingston. We gave the new ones to the folks at the infirmary and took their dirty, old mattresses out to be bleached, soaped and scrubbed. For two weeks, we flipped them over and over, cleaning them inside and out, drying them off in the sun and fresh air. By the end of the process, they were fresh and clean, with only a few dips here and there to remind people of their former life. We took these "new" mattresses, along with brand new sheets to the little board homes of our kids. And then we got to watch as these kids jumped up and down at the thought of having their own beds. Nothing gets thrown away in the world of ACE. We do everything we can to make things last forever. In more ways than one.

We ask the families where they get their food. We get all kinds of answers to that question. Sometimes they share with neighbors. Or they have goats and chickens close by. Many families take it meal by meal. Sometimes we help them plant a garden. We ask them whether they have any regular income. There are all kinds of answers to this one too. When we can, we try to help them with job networking. Lots of people in Jamaica have training or experience in the hospitality business. These conversations can lead to jobs, with us or people we know. Sometimes they lead to business loans or building projects. Our child sponsorship staff, mostly comprised of Jamaicans, has learned to navigate these conversations with a lot of wisdom and a lot of grace. They hear the needs. They hear when people are trying. They hear when people are making up the truth because the real truth is too hard to admit out loud. They hear when people are really hurting. They get to see the way these homes affect the kids they serve at the school.

These relationships give us a chance to spend some time in the heart of the real system—the home. Whether standing at the doorway of a makeshift home or standing in a schoolyard, we're there to bring peace to places of chaos. We are there to protect the defenseless and to invite the children into the presence of Christ, just as he himself did despite the protest of the sensible adults who thought there were more important things to do. The children are not only the future of the island but they are a crucial part of the present. We want to make their reality different today so that tomorrow just keeps getting better.

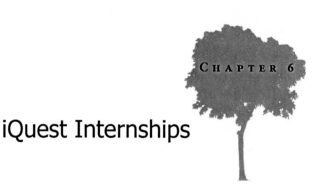

iQuest Internships

We ask them to study Scripture
with us all summer.

2010 iQuest interns with Marla and Allen

While most Americans are taking things a little slower in the summer, relaxing poolside and sipping sweet tea, ACE is ramping up to a high-octane pace. We host mission trips year-round but the majority of them, particularly for students, happen in the summer. To help us through the season, we make the most of an incredibly valuable and overlooked resource—the young adult intern. Every summer, through our iQuest internships, we host young people who spend 75 days with us, following the call to serve and leading others to do the same.

We see this internship as a chance for God to do great things in kids, who are often in a season of life when they're trying to figure out what kinds of adults they want to be. They're wrestling with leaving behind the life of their childhood and making their faith their own. For many of these young people, they are still in the process of defining their value systems. There are some difficulties in working with this crowd: they are prone to making decisions emotionally and they can get frustrated when their efforts reach an obstacle or a dead end. We provide them plenty of chances to grow in wisdom and in perseverance.

Personally, I get excited about the chance to shape their worldview to match the way God sees the world. We ask them to study scripture with us all summer.

They are mentored and challenged in their spiritual walks. We talk ethics—I can't tell you how many conversations we've had about why bootlegging music and media is also called "stealing." For many of them, they just haven't taken the time to sort out what kind of people they want to be and we get the chance to do that in an environment where questions of character come up every day.

We ask them to completely and fully give their lives away during their time with us, to learn how to give to other people. This is a chance for them to understand what it means to lead people and to develop the skill sets that may just be showing up in them as they get ready to enter the working world.

In fact, our iQuest internship is so formative that it's turned into a great place for us to build into people who have the potential to join us for longer periods as staff. Staffing can be a tricky when your ministry is in a place so many people have only been to for vacation. Frequently, we get staff inquisitions from people who are looking to escape their regular lives or who have unrealistic pictures of what full-time life in Jamaica looks like. By offering internship positions, we have a place to build our core values into people and a place for them to discern whether they are truly called or just trying to get away.

Amber

Amber was one of these young people. She was trying to find her place and figure out her future.

Like many young adults, she was also trying to figure out what it meant to establish her own life outside of her family and whatever expectations they might have for her. Although it's hard to tell now, when she came to us, she struggled with confidence and a fear of failure. To her credit, I think she knew she needed some adventure and we certainly can provide that.

She thought she might want to do medical work. She was interested in missions work or maybe ministry. She only knew she wanted to do something different. She came here for one of our short-term trips and found herself stretched and broken and wanting more. She went from a short-term trip to an intern to stateside staff to full-time staff with ACE. She now leads our iQuest program and our Education efforts.

She helps with our child sponsorship program and our education initiatives. For Amber, every day is a chance for her to see the way God provides the tools and gifts we all need to serve the world. She has learned the secret of ACE—how to take things as far as you can, given your own heart and skills and then prayerfully wait for God to fill in the gap between what you have to offer and what the day requires. In the chaotic environment of the primary schools, Amber brings a peaceful presence as she helps kids build their reading skills and listens to their stories.

She's seen some of the peace she carries become a part of the schools. She's also built trust and respect with the people of St. Mary. She gets called "Auntie" a lot when she arrives at the school, (a title of endearment for those who care for and respect children).

In Jamaica, the people will often warn each other of a stranger among them. If you walk through the streets as a white person, you will hear the warnings around you as Jamaicans shout "white people" to alert others. It's a reminder of just how "other" we are to them sometimes. It's a testament to Amber's role here that one day as she rode through town on her way to school, someone issued a "white girl" warning and someone else shouted, "That's not 'a white girl.' That's Amber."

Morgan

Morgan was trying to find her way too.

When she came to ACE, she was trying to recover from ministry wounds, along with dealing with chronic physical pain. She needed to know that she was capable of doing great things. She also came on some short-term trips and joined us for the iQuest program. She loved seeing students' lives changed as they served together. But even more than that, Morgan fell in love with Jamaica itself. She started caring just as much, if not more, for the locals she was serving. Everything around her in Jamaica started looking more and more beautiful. Before long, she decided to call it home.

Morgan now leads our Green Life Farm efforts.

She helps us build gardens for our sponsored families. She also resources and works with our farming partners. She has learned to speak the common language of farming and loves building relationships with people based on conversations about God's world and God's provisions for us in creation.

She didn't come to us with a resume filled with farming experience, but once again God filled in the gaps. Morgan spent time with farmers in the States and became an organic farm specialist. Eventually, through the support of an ACE supporter, Morgan earned her Master Gardener Certification through Clemson University. Google helped too. She freely confesses that "on the spot" internet research has been crucial to her farming career. God redeems technology too.

We live and work far away so we know that many of the relationships we build at ACE are temporary. People may only be with us for a couple weeks, or a summer, or they may just live in our world once in a while. We also know that when visitors from the U.S. or Canada spend time with us, they often return home ready to serve and do life differently because of their intersection with us. God only needs a moment to do great things. And more often than not, those moments are strong enough to build things that last and that transcend geographical barriers. Our family table is wide and we like it.

A walk home from school with Amber

CHAPTER 7

Health

```
When God guides a vision, sometimes even a
wrong turn can be redeemed into the exact
right turn. And sometimes broken bones can
lead to healing no one could have imagined.
```

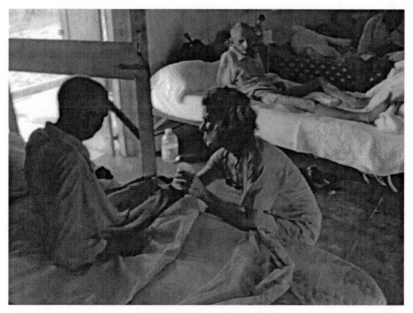

Human touch is everything

I found myself playing ambulance for a Jamaican neighbor who had broken his leg during a soccer match. Badly. We needed to get him to the hospital quickly. But I took a wrong turn. It's easy enough to do around here with the roads twisting and the scattered signs hidden by overgrown trees. We actually ended up in a place that is strategically hidden away from the rest of the community. We only made it there by accident. Instead of a hospital, I ended up at the local "poor house" or the Infirmary. "Poor houses" are a leftover from the colonial days.

Every parish in Jamaica has one because a long time ago the Queen said they should. They were started as a respite for soldiers who served in the royal military. They became a place for people with nowhere else to go. Imagine merging a nursing home, mental health facility and hospice center into one location and you have an idea of the Infirmary.

I was familiar with "poor houses" already. When I lived in the mountains of Jamaica, in Manchester, I used to visit the Infirmary often. I'm pretty sure I was the only person who was ever there voluntarily. Anyone else was only there out of duress, whether they were working there or dying there. I learned that it was an incredibly strategic place to bring the presence of Christ. While many people there were physically falling apart, I realized many of them still had their minds and they were filled with life and stories to tell. There was a chance I could be the last face they saw before they met God. I knew they were uniquely open and interested in the true story of Jesus, a story that takes on entirely new life in the presence of real suffering and death. I knew how we often become like children again as we age, with all the vulnerability and helplessness of newborns.

I had grown up around the dying process. I was strangely comfortable standing in the gateway to eternity. My grandmother earned the family's very first college degree in embalming so spending time in Florida with my grandparents meant spending time at their funeral home business.

Of course, when you are just visiting, funeral homes can take on a whole other tone: I can remember hiding in caskets when I played. But I also remember learning to treat death with respect and I remember learning how death led people to think about forever.

But when I took that wrong turn into the "poor house" some 15 years ago, I did not find a place that treated the dying with any kind of care or dignity. There was no security around the two buildings so patients were vulnerable to outsiders coming in and taking advantage of them. The conditions were treacherous, with dirty beds and filthy showers and very little food or water. The patients were dying in the most disgraceful way possible, as easy targets, with no protection or peace. The underpaid, under-resourced staff seemed to feel helpless. Again, this was a part of a much bigger broken system. They provided minimal support, leaving the patients to starve and shrink away at the end of their lives. There were younger patients too. They were usually abandoned by boys' homes or hospitals, who were maybe only brought there because of some mental illness, doomed to live longer lives in a place meant for people's final days.

> I knew immediately though that the wrong turn had to lead us somewhere.

The thread of justice which ran through me as a child showed up. Every impulse in me wanted to stand up for the weak and defend the Infirmary patients. Defend the moments of suffering and finality. I didn't know what we could do but I knew we were going to do something. I was hoping we could find a way to bring the gifts of the Spirit of God into this place of suffering. If any place in the world could use some love, joy, peace, patience, kindness, goodness, faith, gentleness and self-control, it was this one.

Like a lot of our outreach programs, we started our work just by showing up. I made regular visits. I started bringing teams there. We brought Jamaican comfort food, juicy patties, and juice, insuring the patients would at least get some sustenance. We started trying to mentally and emotionally revive the patients who spent their days hiding their heads under towels just waiting for life to be over. We turned the radio on, hoping that the songs could stimulate memories the way they so often do. I thought if they couldn't yet move or leave this place physically, at least they could come to life and dance in their mind.

Some of the patients seemed to be overmedicated or wrongly medicated to dull the symptoms of their mental illnesses. With so many patients and so few staff, it was difficult to deal with the possible aggression that can come with mental illness. There were many patients who were bedridden but not because they had to be— they just had lost any reason to move for a very long time so their muscles and senses had all atrophied. The crucial physical therapy that has become standard in America's best hospitals and care facilities is a luxury in poverty. We started giving them reasons to move and think and feel again. We engaged them in mental stimulation, getting them to sit up and talk to us. We found out some of them had been professionals, parents and thriving people before they came to the Infirmary. They had just lost the will to try anymore. We started taking them to the beach and helping them to relive their past and engage with their present. There is nothing quite as complicated or beautiful as 25 teenagers taking 80 infirmary patients to the beach.

Infirmary men passing the day away with dominoes

One of our other regular practices was to hold "love and rubs" with the teams that visited the Infirmary. We encouraged teams to offer the patients lotion and then apply it to their dry skin. We hoped that this might be a way for people to receive affection and to be reminded of their value and their humanity. This practice goes back to my grandmother always telling me to connect to aging people through touch. She had a brilliant theory which I'm sure is true: Younger people don't usually want to be reminded of the aging process so they tend to avoid getting too close to people who show them their inevitable future. No one wants to be reminded of their own mortality so they avoid addressing the mortality of others. She always told me this could be isolating for people and to make sure and reach out whenever I had the chance.

Much of what we do at the Infirmary is simple—we make sure people have the necessities of life. I think the necessities extend beyond food and water, which we provide, but also affection, movement, communication.

I know these visits to the Infirmary stretch our teams. They are used to suffering being kept in its place, often out of sight. As long as aging, hurting and dying take place somewhere out of our line of sight, we are free to go along in our self-centered cocoons. Until it's us. Or someone we love and then our worlds come crashing down. Sometimes it's difficult for people who experience too much empathy or who whose empathy drives them right to action. It can be difficult for people who want to fix things to see people in a situation with no obvious solution. It can be tough for our medical teams to see the insufficient care. It challenges people to literally get their hands dirty, but also to let their hearts get a little broken. We know it pushes many people emotionally to see the depths of suffering here. Of course, part of what we ask teams to do is to be ready to do more than they think they can. The Infirmary certainly challenges some people's limits on how much they can take.

We ask our teams to push themselves because we know God will meet them there. If they will just reach out and touch a person who seems untouchable. If they will sit and talk with a patient who seems to be resistant or shut down. Or read the Bible with someone who's been trying to shut out the light and the world for days on end. God will join them in that work and take them further than they think they can go.

We've gotten to see some great things in Jamaica and in our American teams since we started "showing up" at the Infirmary.

Over time, ACE has supplied the Infirmary many physical renovations. We provided the patients with the brand new mattresses, along with bedding. We've built a security fence and improved the road, hoping more people might decide to visit. Even bugs will have a hard time getting in since we gave them screens for the windows and doors to keep them out. We've supplied patients with wheelchairs. We've done some maintenance on their plumbing and electrical systems. We've painted walls and grown a garden, hoping to bring some beauty into the darkness. We've established better relationship with the Jamaican staff there and when we can, we've tried to find ways to serve them as well.

> I know walking in there that we have established
> an authority as a presence there.

Our faithful visits have raised the level of accountability and the level of care around the Infirmary. They know we are going to show up three days a week, at least, at about the same time in the afternoon. After years of our "showing up," somewhere in my files, I have a rare letter of appreciation from the Jamaican Minister of Health for ACE's improvements at the facility.

Any change we've been able to see at the Infirmary can be attributed to our attempt to live out the Mango Tree Gospel—to foster deep and lasting relationships and to practice faithfulness. Before we begin any new outreach effort, we ask whether we can commit to doing it for the next ten years. This long-term filter makes all the difference in our discussions of new ideas and opportunities. It helps us to sort out what is worth the effort and energy required to start something new. It commits us to working through the inevitable struggles that will come when a project reaches the six-month mark, or even the two-year slump. It enables us to imagine and process potential and real failures. I know this stands in contrast to the experimental culture in America, where churches and ministries, along with business and entrepreneurs, are encouraged to "just try things."

This can lead to great discoveries, but it can also lead to a lot of starting and stopping. It can also damage trust. In our community, we feel called to build, rather than experiment. That's not to say we don't try to be innovative, but we always make sure that our innovations are coupled with faithfulness.

The ten-year question also helps us to make sure that we are staying inside of a bigger story and drawing lines between our brilliant ideas and God's bigger plans. Your vision has to be strong if you're going to sustain it for a ten-year minimum.

In addition to programs, the ten-year question also changes our relationships. For our part, we hope to build lasting relationships with churches, partners and volunteers. We want to be in ministry together for a long time. This opens ACE and our partners up to the same kinds of vulnerabilities found in deeper relationships.

The look says it all

You know more about your partner's flaws when you're ten years into a marriage than you do on the first date. Eventually, if we are committed, we will see each other's weaknesses. People might figure out that I can be kind of loud sometimes and opinionated almost all of the time. I might start to notice the dysfunctions in their organizations. I might (absolutely) call out their short attention span if they come to us looking for a trendy way to serve. Over time, we will get to see each other's humanity—you can't hide that for very long. But I think all of this is good. God uses broken people and fortunately, that's all of us. We might as well get to see and know that in each other.

But trying to emulate the deep roots of a mango tree doesn't always make sense to those who treat serving God as one entertainment option out of many. We have people come through ACE who are here looking for adventure or a quality Facebook profile picture. They are coming here to have their own needs met. Even though it looks like they're serving others, they're doing it to say they did it, not to make an actual investment. But for those who resist this trend, the ones who come back year after year, they get to see the same child they tutored in second grade make her way to fifth grade. They get to know the patients at the Infirmary. If volunteers will join us in the practice of faithfulness, we think there's some long-term fruit for them to bear. In fact, many of them do—87% of our volunteers are making return trips. They are repeat offenders and we'll take them anytime.

For all of our emphasis in ACE on sustainability, our ministry at the Infirmary is our only "unsustainable" work. We know the work we do there has a different kind of lasting value. It doesn't cost us much funding but donors and churches rarely think to give specifically to our work at the Infirmary. It doesn't have the same feeling of "investment" and hope that giving to kids has. But I still think it's a place where we can have the biggest impact. And often the final impact. I also believe it's an investment in the future—just a different kind. We are often there as people face their death and we get to be present in the final moments, hopefully reminding them of Christ's invitation and love so they might make their final home with him.

In addition to being present in death, we've seen patients come to life too. From time to time, our teams are greeted by Sylvia, who greets them with a song and a smile and asks them to sign her Bible. Many of our teams have gotten to know Richard, a young man with some limitations, who will spend the majority of his life on this hillside watching people age and die around him, but who somehow still manages to be filled with joy.

We see volunteers push through their discomfort and serve these strangers with warmth and compassion. I've seen grown men cradle frail older folks as they try to serve them juice and an afternoon snack. I've experienced those moments when two strangers who don't understand anything about the other's way of life suddenly find something to talk about, to bring them both back to life.

I often get letters from people when they return home saying their time here helped them to appreciate the elderly in their own lives. People return home and spend time with grandparents, having learned the value of affection and conversation with other generations. I also hear a lot of people who say their time at the Infirmary reminds them of the reality of death, causing them to evaluate where they are in their life.

Serving at the Infirmary also raises questions about suffering for many of our American visitors. While ACE is doing everything we can to improve the conditions, there is only so much any of us can do for the actual process of death and dying. For people who have not seen death yet in their own life, it can be difficult to face in this environment. Seeing a room full of people in physical pain, waiting for their life to end on the top of a hill in 90 degree heat, complete with 100% humidity, has a way of making people wonder where God is and why this happens. After a day at the Infirmary, people usually spend the evening sitting around the hotel pool trying to process some of life's most important questions.

For my part in conversations on suffering, I try to remind people the character of God does not change.

> God is not indifferent to the pain in
> this little corner of Jamaica.

God grieves the conditions at the Infirmary. God cares about the little old lady hiding from the world under her towel. God mourns for the man who has given up on his own life because the world has given up on him. God sees all the people who walk by the street to the Infirmary without ever giving a thought to the people who are suffering there.

As we see over and over again in the stories of the Old Testament, God mourns and laments the choices humans make. Paul explains this is in writing to the Romans, how creation is being held hostage in decay and darkness:

"For the creation waits with eager longing for the revealing of the children of God; for the creation was subject to futility, not of its own will but by the will of the one who subjected it, in hope that the creation itself will be set free from its bondage to decay and will obtain the freedom of the glory of the children of God. We know that the whole creation has been groaning in labor pains until now; and not only creation but we ourselves, who have the first fruits of the Spirit, groan inwardly while we wait for adoption, the redemption of our bodies." (Romans 8.19-23)

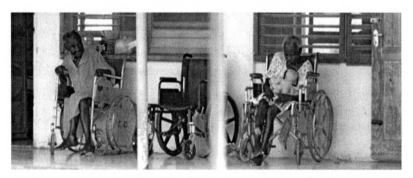

Of course, the promise of God is that we will know freedom someday and there will be a new creation. There will be release from suffering and a balm for all kinds of pain. But for now, there are faithful ways we can respond to the suffering we see.

We can respond with gratitude. If the world is not the world God imagined it could be, and if God is grieved over the state of things, I want to use my voice and my life to refresh the heart of God and bring God joy. I try to wake up in the morning and see the world not only for what it is but what it could be. What if we all recognized all the places and ways that the love of God breaks through the mess we've made of things? I want to praise God for the rising of the sun and the rhythm of the ocean waves. I thank God for the moments when people smile or feel joy in the midst of pain.

Every time I hear an awful story of something going on near me, I ask the same question I asked when I first took that wrong turn to the Infirmary: "Is there anything I can do to stop this or help this?" It's not an easy question to ask and it's almost always a difficult question to answer.

There are times when I know there is no answer. There are stories that are too hard or too far away and I'm left feeling small and crushed under the weight of them. It's a necessary moment; we all need to see and feel our weaknesses sometimes. And of course, even when the answer is "yes," when there is very clearly something I can do, or something ACE can do, it's still God working through us. It's a strange and beautiful thing when God allows us to become the answer to our own prayers.

When faced with the very present reality of physical suffering in St. Mary, we have seen God do great things through ACE as a response to our prayers and pleas.

Medical doctor writing a prescription

Living the Mango Tree Gospel and planning for ten years of faith-fulness also led us to offering medical and dental clinics year-round out in the communities around us. I started noticing how many of my

neighbors I was hearing about dying in their thirties from simple cur-
able diseases. I heard of people dying from infections, and ulcers, and
diabetes. Again, I knew something needed to be done. As I researched
foreign medical work, I realized how little interest there was in long-term
care. Return trips were rare at the time. Talking to doctors and nurses
who took part in short-term trips, I learned that they were pained by
the lack of follow-up and long-term care. For all the good these groups
could do in the moment, there were no wellness plans, no means for
prevention. The short-term system also catered to self-interests—people
who wanted to make one trip to say they did it but weren't inclined to
personal investment called out to medical professionals for help. Dr.
Steve Guy, an obstetrician/gynecologist from Dayton, Ohio, who has
bonus leadership experience as the father to eight children, joined me.
He has an entrepreneurial spirit and a deep passion for helping people. I
first met Dr. Guy when he came along on a dental trip with several dental professionals from Troy, Ohio. Not only was he the only non-dental
person on the trip, he was the only male. I knew he had to be something
special to join 12 women on a cross-country trip. My suspicions were
confirmed one day when we were holding a clinic at a hotel and were
interrupted by a heavy rainstorm and leaky roof. The team was huddled
under tarps, bored and waiting for the storm to pass, when Dr. Guy
said something no one really expected, "Why don't I look at everyone's
uterus?" In some situations, maybe that would be strange but he had an
ultra-sound machine and we really had nothing better to do. As he ran
the monitor over all of us gathered there, he also offered commentary.
He was able to "read" everyone's story and figure out whether they had
children, how they sized up to other people. No matter how it sounds, I
promise it was a good time. And I knew then that Dr. Guy was cut out
for the mission field. I knew he had a contagious energy, could roll with
whatever was put in front of him and was willing to cross any professional barriers or expectations that other people might have. Before he
left, I gave him a homemade business card with his name and "Medical
Missions Director" written on it. I presented it to him as if God himself
had dropped the card from the sky and was calling him to serve with
us. He took me (and God) up on the offer.

> Together, we stumbled through the beginning
> of our medical clinic program.

We paid attention to patterns as we served in those first years and kept track of frequent diagnoses. We built up a pharmacy and worked with the Jamaican Ministry of Health to secure medical permits. We were also able to join with them to use the clinic buildings they had in several communities. Like most medical efforts, this one came with some bureaucratic limitations but eventually, we were building something to last.

ACE now brings in doctors, dentists, nurses, physical therapists—pretty much anyone willing to care for the needs of the people here. We manage six clinics in different communities and return there every 90 days or so. Because of this consistency, we often end up being able to treat the same patients. Again, many of the professionals who come to help on short-term trips end up making repeated visits so we are able to offer long-term care. We've been able to build relationships among our volunteers, but also with Jamaican health care workers. Eventually, Dr. Guy passed off leadership of the medical efforts but he still makes regular trips to St. Mary and the program keeps growing under the direction of Dr. Ron Eaker. If you go up into the mountains of rural Jamaica and ask some of the people who their physician is, they'll probably tell you it's a doctor from Dayton, Ohio or Augusta, Georgia.

We offer whatever help we can during these clinics. We screen for diabetes. We serve a wide-range of problems, from sinusitis to STD's. We are able to refer people who may have serious or life-threatening conditions. When possible, we try to direct patients to whatever quality local care may be available so that local doctors continue to draw in patients and income. We offer people medicine if we can and almost always some conversation, education and prayer.

When we started offering these clinics, we weren't exactly sure where they would lead. Our very first dental clinic consisted of a collection of beach chairs set up in a small grove of banana trees. It was a far cry from the comfy chairs and easy listening radio of an American dental visit. I suppose we could have set up a stereo playing Michael Bolton but I'm not sure it would have comforted anyone. We had more than 300 people show up. When you offer free medical care in Jamaica, apparently word travels fast. We learned the power of what they call the "bush telegram." News travels through neighbors as effectively as a Tweet or a Facebook status. We served them from breakfast to sundown. Our dentists and assistants were pulling teeth right and left and collecting them in buckets (Seriously, Jamaicans really, really like sugar).

Roy has a toothache

One of my favorite images from that very first clinic was of our five-foot tall dentist pulling the tooth of a six-foot tall Rastafarian. Rastafarians are peace-loving, gentle souls who apparently don't tell you when you're getting ready to pull the wrong tooth. In the frenzy of the day, our dentist pulled a tooth that needed pulling but was not actually numbed. Take that in for a minute and spend some time imagining what it would be like if you went to the dentist and he pulled a tooth without the help of Novocain. The Rasta man just sat there strongly and quietly and then calmly asked after, "What about the tooth where you injected the shot?" I suppose in a community where suffering is just living, a little tooth pain must feel like it's hardly worth mentioning.

Looking forward, our next ten-year commitment in medical outreach is to create a Wellness Center. We want to find a way to provide high quality urgent care to the community, along with offering preventative education and care. The holistic approach to health is already established as a way of life in Jamaica so we want to meet them where they are and capitalize on the interest here in natural care. For their lack of access to medicines and treatment options, Jamaica is wealthy with herbs, plants and natural solutions. Sometimes people just need help seeing the resources in front of them. There's nothing quite like this in Jamaica so we're cooperating with the local health care industry to create a genuinely "Jamerican" program. Our hope is to turn this center into a "For-Profit" endeavor that will create local jobs and be able to sustain itself as a business. It's a big dream for this community but it's a dream that makes a whole lot of sense. As of print, the location has been scoped out, the permits secured and the plans are made with the goal of treating people by 2015.

There is a lot made in the Gospel stories of Jesus' ability to heal the physical ailments of the people suffering around him. He showed his power by being able to restore sight to the blind, mobility to the lame, voices to the mute. Miracles like these are certainly possible. But there is another kind of miracle that we get to see around ACE all the time: When God works through a person who has invested a large portion of his or her life and resources to become a doctor, dentist, or medical professional and then uses those skills to treat the poor and the under-resourced. It's a beautiful thing to see God honor the lives of these professionals who are using their gifts for something other than a profit or recognition.

We see healing all the time. We see healing when our volunteers take the Infirmary patients to the beach, forgetting all about their own need for fun, and guiding the patients into the water and sand. Healing happens when our nurses take the time to listen to the hurts and aches of people who have been bearing pain for a very long time. Or when Jamaicans walk away from our care smiling and carrying lighter burdens. The world may be groaning, and it might not yet be what God dreams it can be, but when God's at work, even broken legs can lead to great healing.

CHAPTER 8

On Healing

"Now to him who is able to do immeasurably more than all we ask or imagine, according to his power that is at work within us."
(Ephesians 3.20)

Deacon Ellis was an elder in one of the churches where I served in the mountains as a choir director. He also lived at the bottom of my street so occasionally my pickup truck was also his taxi to church. He lived in a small board house with an outdoor kitchen where he and his wife cooked together. He was only in his 50s when he suddenly started looking 1,000 years old. He went to a doctor in the capital city of Kingston and he was diagnosed with cancer. When you don't have access to money for treatment, cancer is pretty much a death sentence. The window of hope offered by chemotherapy and radiation was closed to Deacon Ellis.

He deteriorated quickly. He seemed to shrink as time passed and his muscles atrophied. Death is a painful process without painkillers. For a time, he was taking aspirin for a pain most Americans would get to treat with morphine.

Despite his frailty, the people of the church saw God at work. Late one night, after a Wednesday night church service, I got a phone call from the pastor declaring God was going to heal Deacon Ellis the next day. Thankfully, it was a phone call so I could hide my skeptical face. I must admit I was faithless when it came to the possibility of healing. My upbringing and my learned understanding of God didn't allow for these kinds of miracles. I was already grieving and now I was concerned that he and his family were heading towards a shattering disappointment.

But I joined the prayers over Deacon Ellis. Not knowing what to say, I was a silent observer. I tried to match their hope and faith. The elders of this tiny church always reminded me of Jesus' disciples. They were tradesmen too. Men who were probably better at masonry than reading and writing. Filled with faith and ready to follow wherever Jesus led. The next day as the men prayed, I put my hands on Deacon Ellis' leg. I remember the pastor proclaiming: "Elder Ellis—this is the day that the Lord has made! Are you ready to be healed? You'll be eating dinner tonight!" With this exclamation, I figured the situation had just gone from bad to worse. But despite my skepticism, within seconds of the first prayers, I felt heat radiating from where I placed my hand on his leg. Then I started feeling movement, as if the tissues and muscles that had fallen apart were coming back to life. All I could think of was Ezekiel and his dry bones story, how God brings life out of what the world has destroyed. The scrunched up, frail, shrunken body of Mr. Ellis was growing in strength and he was breathing and resurrecting right in front of us.

Before long our prayers became songs and our petitions became praises. Mr. Ellis joined the singing and the weeping and the thanking. I felt awkward and embarrassed, like a traitor to God with insignificant faith. I realized I didn't know God nearly as well as I thought I did. I decided I probably needed to do some reading on healing. I started searching, looking for challenges to my conservative and limited understanding of the work and movement of God. I became aware of my own tendency—maybe shared with a lot of others—to relegate these acts of God to the crazy corners of faith. The resurrection of Deacon Ellis brought my faith back to life and I became determined to know God first hand rather than just believing the descriptions from other people.

The next day Deacon Ellis was out of his deathbed and dancing in the streets. The people in the town were shocked to see him. If I had to guess, I'd say there were 50 people or so who came to believe in the true God because they saw God heal this man who believed in Him. Every Sunday, the good Deacon would get up and tell his story of how close he was to death and how God brought him back to life. It was a powerful testimony that reminded me of all the great accounts of miracles in the book of Acts done for the sake of unbelieving hearts.

A year or so later, I was driving Mr. Ellis home from church in the truck. I told him I would see him the next day. As he stepped out of my truck, he collapsed and the minute he hit the dirt, he was dead. It was sudden and surprising. His wife rushed out from their house. We all realized his time had come, not when expected but when God and Deacon Ellis were ready for him to be home.

As I was driving away later, I wondered why God would go to all that trouble of healing Mr. Ellis only to have him die a short while after. But I suppose it had to happen eventually. We all have a time when we'll die and move on. His quick and sudden death ruled out cancer as the cause. The doctor thought it was a heart attack. The best explanation I could think of is that God wanted to do a great work in Mr. Ellis. He needed it to be dramatic. He needed it to be clear in Mr. Ellis' life and death that God was the one with the power. My days in Jamaica have brought me closer and closer to understanding Paul when he says God can "accomplish abundantly far more than all we can ask or imagine." (Ephesians 3.20)

CHAPTER 9

Discipleship

But if I have to choose between efficient and effective, I'm going for effective.

It's a great irony that many of the world's fastest sprinters come from Jamaica. This is not a fast island. Life moves slowly here. It's part of what makes Jamaica the perfect place for busy tourists to escape the clock and relax for a while. It's also part of what makes life difficult if you are a driven, Type A, multi-tasker. Here, every little errand or interaction becomes an exercise in patience. I constantly find myself trying to walk a line between trying to get things done and trying to keep pace with the people and their life's rhythms. It's true every time I go to the hardware store. It's also true every time we try to lead the people of St. Mary into a saving relationship with Jesus.

Sometimes people see all the things ACE is involved in—the medical work, the education initiatives, the business loans—and they wonder where evangelism happens. They don't immediately see the connection between our role in the community and leading people to Jesus. But this connection is at the heart of everything we do. Ultimately, we are here to follow the call of Jesus to make disciples (Matt. 28.19-20). But in a place where life, and people, move slower, sometimes this process goes at a different pace than the one driven Americans are accustomed to.

It's incredibly important to us to share the character and the story of Christ through relationships. And in a culture that is slow to trust, with as many social barriers as there can be between ACE and the people of St. Mary, this can take a lot of patient years of building and nurturing.

From time to time, we host church groups who want to walk through the streets and spread evangelism tracts or preach on the street corners.

They have a point, I suppose. Getting people to say "yes" to Jesus after a five-minute conversation would certainly be more efficient than 25 years of investing in the community and building local credibility and local leadership.

But if I have to choose between efficient and effective, I'm going for effective. Also, I'm not sure that choosing Christ should ever be a five-minute decision. This seems to be more of an American method than any global understanding of conversion. I believe making a life-changing decision to spend your life following hard after Jesus should take some time, some research, some thought. It's the most important decision of our lives. If your son or daughter went out on a first date, you would never welcome the date into your home and begin the conversation by asking if this was the person your child was going to marry. (Usually parents hope this first date never, ever shows up again! But that's beside the point). The point is that true salvation often takes time. Life-altering decisions need room and time. Especially in a culture that doesn't move at break-neck American speed (unless it's on the race track).

But just because life in Jamaica moves slower, doesn't mean we don't move with intention.

Every relationship, every connection we make in the world of ACE is an opportunity for God to show up. We see this in our relationships with the local school administrators. Or as we treat people in the medical clinics. When we run into kids on the street. We build trust with them. We listen to them. And often, over time, they start to understand that we are driven by the love of God and they want in.

Even with our visiting volunteers from America and Canada, people who may or may not be coming as part of a church group, their time with ACE may be the first time they are encountering the real Christ. We have people who come on trips who haven't yet come to a point of decision to trust God and follow Jesus. But when they come to Jamaica, they are away from their cubicles, and away from daily distractions. They are being pushed to the limits of their skills and comfort. It makes sense that people can hear God better when they're here since they may finally be listening. The ocean view and mountains certainly don't hurt.

As an interdenominational group, we are uniquely positioned to cut through any peripheral issues people might have with churches or in relationships and get right to the Gospel. In our work and in our language, we want to be an authentic representation of the great salvation God is offering people through faith. We want people to catch glimpses through us of God at work so they can return home with a desire to learn more and more. For anyone who comes through ACE as part of a short-term trip, I offer for them to join me for online Bible study, hoping to return the gift I received from friends who did the same for me.

We've had practical atheists and agnostics come to faith during their time with us and we've had a lot of short-term relationships become longer-term.

No matter how long people are with us, we are honored to play some small part in the larger story God is writing in people's lives. The Apostle Paul told the church at Corinth in 1 Corinthians 3.6: "I planted, Apollos watered, but God gave the growth." In hosting trips, we get to play a part and trust that we are joining God in working on people's hearts.

I am convinced that God often uses ACE to reveal the core of people. We see this in our visiting groups and in the locals who become a part of our mission. Any pretension or falsehood fades away when they interact with us. I have the chance to do the same thing for them that God did for me in the mirror—to show them their true selves and to show them a vision for who they could be. This is the heart of our work but it's also the work of the Gospel, whether it happens over a five-minute conversation on the street or a tangled ten-year relationship.

One summer, I hosted the daughter of a friend, a high school junior who had developed a love for darkness and a hatred for herself. She came to us with two suicide attempts behind her. During her time here, I learned she had let evil slip into her life in seemingly small ways—a taste for graphic fiction about killers and killing, a place in fleeting "goth" culture, pagan idols in her room for "decoration." They all opened her up to the authority of the lowly "prince of this world" as Jesus calls him. But through prayer and service and hearing the truth from Scripture, she left here as a follower and a lover of Jesus.

Sometimes the changes come later as visitors only fully absorb what they learned here when they get home. We had an intern once whose sarcasm and bitterness made me want to put him back on an airplane almost as soon as he arrived. He was young, living in a turbulent family, and he disagreed with everything we did and let us know it. I let him stay, hoping God would use ACE to shake his world a little. When he left, I even told him some kind of "shake" was coming. I knew he would know loss someday and he might need us again. Two years later he wrote me apologizing for his arrogance and for causing trouble. He was losing his mom and struggling with faith. His time with us had shored up his faith even after he was long gone.

I've also gotten to see this process of coming to faith in several of the Jamaicans who are actually on staff here at ACE. We try to open up as many jobs to folks from here in St. Mary as we can. Many Jamaicans are trained and qualified to serve in the hospitality industry so they're able to work for the hotel. If they're not trained but we see potential, then we train them ourselves. They also work with our education and child sponsorship programs. We do not hire Christians exclusively—most of our Jamaican hires come from relationships with people we already know and trust. Even this process moves slowly by American standards. The hiring process all over the island is heavily dependent on recommendations. In a world without a lot of degrees and resume building opportunities, your character and reputation serve as your cover letter. Everyone we hire is hired on a 90-day trial basis. Over this time, they shadow our Jamaican staff and they get to hear the Jamaican staff tell them our story—why we're here and what really matters. We also look for healthy patterns in their work and their life— whether they tell the truth, whether they show up when they say they will show up. When poverty dominates a culture, even teaching basic job performance and ethics becomes means for discipleship and a way to train people to honor God with their lives.

ACE's most-senior employee is Mr. Myers. He was actually the security guard for the Tradewinds hotel before it became Galina Breeze. His own story goes from the island of Jamaica to the sugar cane farms of the U.S. and back to the little security hut along the Jamaican shore. He is now a "guard" in all kinds of ways. He uses his farming expertise to help plant gardens in our sponsored families' homes and is also a part of our education initiatives. He is our symbolic grandfather on staff. His role, along with the other men of ACE, is crucial in our ministry. When we try to explain the metaphor of God as "Father" to Jamaicans, they struggle. The Jamaican family system is usually matriarchal with the men living in the background, away from the family, if they are involved at all. Through the strong and safe presence of Mr. Myers, our kids and our friends get to see what a protective Dad might look like.

Brandon modeling a father for a fatherless child

We have other strong men in place too: Brandon first came to us looking for a job as a security guard but it didn't take long before we realized he was qualified for more responsibility. (His story is a great picture of being faithful in small things hoping they will lead to greater things). He had just become a father and eventually he ended up leading our child sponsorship program. Although he is a native Jamaican, he was educated in the United Kingdom. For some Jamaicans who leave the island for education and then return, their time overseas can be a source of pride and condescension towards their community. But not with Brandon. He sees his education and his experience as a gift he was given that needs to be given away. Brandon talks to our sponsored families with a particular kind of grace and dignity. He hears them, sometimes even when they're saying things they won't say out loud. He also has the intangible gift for being respected instantly by children. It's a rare thing but great to see in action. When he first came to serve with us, he was not a Christ-follower but God kept chasing Brandon. Brandon eventually knew he was missing the abundant life offered by Christ and desperately wanted it. Now that he knows the love of God, he leads others in ways that help them walk more like Jesus.

Sometimes members of our staff have been ready to hear the story of Jesus and connect their lives to him for a long time. Sometimes it's a messier process. McGyver (and yes, he can do just about anything with some duct tape, a stapler, and a hairbrush) came to us at a time when his life was out of control. A year into working with ACE, I had to confront him with some hard truths about his life. In order to be who we all knew he could be, I advised him to drop the three extra girlfriends he had in his life and marry the mother of his kids so he could teach his son, and himself, about the freedom that comes from commitment. He wasn't sure about that in the moment. He needed some time.

Three months later, to show he was really serious about faith, he came in and announced he had given his life to Jesus at church and wanted to mark that decision through baptism. He was also ready to marry Prudence and they were the first couple married at Galina Breeze.

Their wedding was a great adventure for us. It got started four hours later than planned which is not unusual in Jamaica although Americans would probably riot over it. The hotel staff all worked for free that day and McGyver contributed his own rams' goat and pig to the feast. We were ready for 100 guests. But then the buses from Kingston and other parts of the island started rolling in. McGyver is a lovable guy who draws people to him, all kinds of people. There were people from his past, which included a stay in prison, and people who were almost certainly packing weapons and liquor. Before long, there were 250 people, some who were armed, ready to be a part of a wedding without enough space or food. We had a problem, Houston. I was worried fights might break out, or at the very least, we would be violating every rule Miss Manners ever gave for proper wedding etiquette. Fortunately, McGyver was able to use the same charm that drew so many people to convince them to settle for drinking their rum and Red Stripe by the pool and miss the dinner. They partied and had a great time and got back on their buses around midnight to head home without incident. It was a crazy day turned beautiful which is often the way God works around here.

We got to see God move in the life of Ms. Shirley, our head cook at the hotel.

When Ms. Shirley came to us, she had to work really hard to smile. She was a single mom who had let the world and broken relationships convince her that she had little to no value in the world. We saw that she had a precious and beautiful heart. We also discovered she could cook like nobody's business and deserved to have her face on the cover of a cookbook. We hoped through her time with ACE, she would learn the truth that God loved her and had a great purpose for her. She had already been with us for two years when the truth sank in for her. She asked to talk to our general manager, they prayed together and Ms. Shirley welcomed the presence of Christ in her life. She said she had never seen people who lived out of faith and wanted that for her life too. Like many of the people we meet who are struggling with poverty and the effects of it on the heart, Ms. Shirley still struggles with wondering if she's good enough but she's an incredibly important person to ACE, Galina Breeze and to God. She's family and often serves as a leader to the younger people who come through her kitchen.

Ms. Shirley

Coach, or Lincoln Small, came to us through soccer (or football as it's known pretty much everywhere but America). Coach's nickname is Thumbscrew, because he's small in stature but a powerful leader. He had been a trainer for a semi-professional referee federation and volunteered with us as a coach for our soccer outreach program. We wanted to reach the young adult men in the community and knew the soccer team in Galina was looking for a sponsor. All we needed was a coach. His coaching skills took our team up in the ranks, even though the soccer board occasionally worked against us because they knew we had access to money. Coach didn't let them stop the team and just kept leading them to victory. Even more than his coaching skills, we saw his commitment and his discipline. We also got to know him as a family man and learned he had been tutoring and discipling his granddaughter who was at the top of her class in every grade. We knew he could help a lot more students as a part of ACE's tutoring program. What we didn't know is that he had secretly wanted to be a part of ACE for a while. Now he's in and he's a respected mentor for the children ACE serves. His athletic discipline translates into structure and guidance for our education efforts in the schools. He tutors at the primary school and is also our truant officer. When kids start missing too many days, he makes a visit to their home to deal with the cause of their absenteeism. Under his watch, attendance at our schools has increased exponentially. Coach talks sometimes about having faith in God and we know the Gospel is making its' way into his heart and his life.

> It's fun to watch how people come
> to find a home with ACE.

Many preachers and church leaders are working so hard to fight against the cycles of violence, illiteracy and idleness, that their messages just end up as lists of *do's* and mostly *don'ts.*

Kim had moved to Jamaica from Canada and had been volunteering at a school in another community. In her fifties, Kim had already "grown her children," as they say in Jamaica for empty-nesters. She heard about our involvement in schools and wanted to be a part. She

is now on staff with us and has been a tremendous help teaching kids to read, even if it is with a slight Canadian accent.

The stories may come slower here but when they come, they're good. In the past, the process of making disciples also presented us with a real struggle. In our work, we often end up introducing people to the freedom and the abundant life offered by Jesus. We get to show and tell the gospel through our hotel and through our partnerships. But ACE didn't have a formal way to disciple and grow the people who decided to follow Jesus through their connection to us.

There are lots of churches here in Jamaica. But they are often steeped in traditional values and practices. Their struggles are not completely different from American mainline churches that have been slow to make changes to style and language. In fact, in many ways, Jamaica is a religious culture. But much like their educational system, their prayers and their understanding of God can become rote and religious instead of alive and personal.

The "memorize and repeat" methods in the classroom also make their way into the sanctuary. People are often taught to just absorb and memorize whatever Scriptures their preachers give them, instead of learning to read the Bible and make it come alive in their own worlds.

When I first made Galina my home, I visited every church within four miles. I remember hearing a lot of Scripture used for purposes other than what they were intended for. Some of this is connected to literacy problems on the island. When most of the Gospel message is reliant on hearsay and not in the actual word of God, things can get messy.

Add to that the simple aesthetics of a traditional Jamaican church experience—the wooden pews and the three-hour long services, complete with babies crying and children running the aisles - and it's easy to see why the younger generation is particularly uninterested in what's happening at the church.

There's also a tremendous spiritual battle going on in our community. Galina is a dark place spiritually speaking. It's home to a number of cults and leaves a lot of room for the "cosmic powers of this present darkness" that Paul talks about in his letter to the Ephesians. (Eph. 6.12)

Many preachers and church leaders are working so hard to fight against the cycles of violence, illiteracy and idleness, that their messages just end up as lists of *do's* and mostly *don'ts*.

To be fair, there are good reasons preachers lean towards preaching against things instead of "for" things. Over the years, this community has seen an influx of deportees who have landed here because of their involvement in terrorist activities or drug trafficking. This has had an "octopus with tentacles" effect as transported criminals started preying on hopeless people and bringing them into their crime circles. Our schools are often broken into and robbed. Even our garden programs are vulnerable to theft, as hungry people steal ripened food, even from our schoolyards. Just recently, the home of a friend of ACE was set on fire, killing a young child and leaving her mom and another three-year old behind with severe burns. When we create jobs for people, it can cause friction in the community as envy and jealousy show up. We've had employees' friends and neighbors cook up schemes to get them fired, possibly hoping to get their job or just out of pure revenge for a life well-lived. These are just stories from the circle of people we know through ACE but the darkness stretches further than we know. This is why we think it's vital we start showing as many people as we can another kind of life.

I had known Pastor Watson for 10 years. He was a successful businessman and pastor who was Jamaican but had also spent some time in America. After a season of corporate success as the Vice-President of a bank, Pastor Watson returned to Jamaica to follow the call of God on his life. When we first started talking about planting this church that only existed in my mind, he was pastoring a storefront church in the capital city of Kingston. He was in no hurry to move to Galina and responded to my pleas by telling me to "just pray." He didn't want to make the move until God had a say in the situation. I should have known by now that God operates independently of my schedule but I guess I had to learn it just one more time. Years later, he made the call: "God says now is the time." He left his church in Kingston with a group of young successors, giving me confidence that he knew not only how to pastor, but how to disciple. Acts Church, ministry partner of ACE, stands out from other churches on the island. People know right away that this isn't church as they've always known it. People dress more casually when they come to Acts Church.

Pastor Winston Watson, an ACE advisory board member, at ACTS church

They hear different music than they heard growing up in church. It sounds more like the stuff they hear on the radio and they like it. Pastor Watson and the other church leaders have to wrestle with many of the same questions as American churches: Can you break from tradition but still honor it? How do you help people understand grace and righteousness at the same time? What is the best way to communicate truth? Should we do the announcements before the message or after? You know, all the important stuff.

But there are unique challenges too. How do you move people toward the word of God when they cannot read it? How do you overcome generations of colonialism and create a genuinely Jamaican incarnation of the church? How do you help people who are surrounded by poverty understand the richness that abounds in life with Christ? Actually, that last one is surprisingly simple. Over and over again, we see the Gospel strike chords that ring so deep and so true, it covers over obstacles and barriers. Somewhere deep down, people know their way towards abundant life and when they start to hear it described, they hunger and thirst for it. They respond to it and arrange their life around it.

ACE coordinator, Kemar, with children in ACE's child sponsorship program

Kemar, who works as a part of ACE's child sponsorship program came to us initially through his involvement with Acts Church. He spent time in a boys' home run by Catholic Sisters. He developed a strong work ethic and was actually trained to be a butcher. But Kemar had an entrepreneurial spirit and wanted to strike out and try new things. As a part of ACE, he started a program to offer Physical Education at our schools, something they did not have the resources or energy to do. Kemar recognizes the great redeeming work of God that this young man who grew up without a father figure now gets to play that role for

the children in this community. His story is one we hop
repeat over and over as Acts Church grows and finds its

We also hope to see more and more transformatioı
and build our

Green Life Children's Village. If we do it right, we think we can affect
the community and change the way people understand family. It's the
ultimate discipleship opportunity. We are in the process of building a
collection of small, single family homes on a piece of land in St. Mary.

Each home will eventually hold up to eight children, along with a
set of house parents. While they are a part of the home, the kids will
learn the basic stuff of life: how to do chores, how to live without the
television on, how to farm and tend a garden, how to respect adults,
how to play nicely with others, how to talk with God. When they reach
the age of 15, our hope is that they will be able to go out into the community with a skilled trade and a wise heart so they can mentor kids
who are in the same place they used to be.

We run into children all the time who have run out of places to go.
We know there are families who would courageously place their children in our village in order to give them a better chance at a sustainable
life. Ultimately, we hope children would leave the Village and return to
help their family with what they learn during their time with us. The
Village will also provide counseling for children: part of the restoration
process involves dealing with the difficult parts of life. We know there
are children in this community who have already seen horrible things
that have the potential to haunt them the rest of their lives.

The Village will be a resource for the community in all kinds of
ways. We hope it will become a model for other parishes on the island.
Children's homes or orphanages run a wide spectrum from adequate
to awful. We think our model could be easily copied and multiply the
redemption process. The holistic health and wellness center will also
be attached to the Village. In addition to caring for people's physical
needs, we also want to extend counseling to those outside the children's
home who may need to carry the healing back to their own homes and
circles of family.

We want to show a whole generation of children that life can be done differently.

We know they can learn how to honor God with their whole lives. To see their lives and this Earth as great gifts to be cared for and treated with love. We want the kingdom of God to come to the parish of St. Mary in the same way it will come someday in heaven.

It's where we think the future of our ministry lies—in this principle of Jesus'—of discipling and training more and more people to show and tell others about the life-giving Gospel. We hope it happens through the work of Acts Church but we are also building it into every aspect of ACE's work. For us, this means training and raising up more and more Jamaicans who can speak the truth to their community with power and authority. It's a more holistic approach to ministry. In order for the kingdom of God to become a reality in St. Mary and for it to be clear that God rules here, people need to live healthy lives. People need to be able to read and communicate. People need to be able to sustain their daily lives with income and daily bread. We believe God cares infinitely about people and we want to join God in the work of loving them.

When Jesus sends out his disciples in Matthew 10, he gives them words to say: "The kingdom of heaven has come near." But he also tells them to "cure the sick, raise the dead, cleanse the lepers, and cast out the demons." Sometimes making disciples means starting with their physical needs. We've been focusing on this aspect of Jesus' teaching for a long time. It's our hope in the coming seasons of ministry to go as deep as we go wide.

The funny thing about a ministry with a focus on sustainability is that your ultimate hope is for the day when you are no longer necessary. Like parents who have done a quality job of preparing their child for an entrance into the world, there's satisfaction when the child doesn't need you anymore. ACE will have done our job when we are no longer needed in the community. We're working towards the day, when because of our work and the momentum of God's church, the schools of St. Mary are helping every child to learn to read. And the local churches and professionals are caring for the sick and the poor. And the craftsman and artisans and parents of our parish can provide for their families.

It's great genius on God's part to build the church in such a way that we will only know our work is done when we are no longer seen as vital and instrumental in the work's survival. If we do this right, the things we build, the roots we cultivate, will live and produce longer than one generation. Mango trees long outlive the people who plant them and the storms that threaten to overtake them. They bear fruit for people the planters never see. We want nothing less for the story of ACE.

Street view of Green Life Children's Village

CHAPTER 10

On Your Help

You may be reading this story because you are already a part of ACE in some way. If so, thank you. Thank you for coming to serve, or writing a check, or sponsoring a child, or praying for our work.

If you are reading this story and aren't a part of ACE, hopefully you are starting to wonder how you can be. We don't want this to be just another story about someone moving to a developing country and trying to make a difference. We want this to be a story that moves people to live differently. Hopefully, you're asking yourself what you can do to keep ACE's work going in Jamaica. How can you help the kingdom of God come to life in St. Mary, Jamaica? If you're asking those questions, I have answers.

Part of why we're telling this story right now is to celebrate the past. After twenty-five years of service, we wanted to celebrate. But we're also looking forward to the future. Specifically, we need your help building our Green Life Children's Village. As you read about in the last chapter, we want to build a place that strengthens families and mentors young people who can grow up to lead in this community. It's the ultimate "green" project, recycling and restoring people. We know this can be an extraordinary work for this community, done by ordinary people, like me, who want to be a part of something bigger than ourselves.

Here's how you can be involved and help us make the Village happen:

1. Get a group of your friends or neighbors together and join us for a week-long trip.

2. The cost of your trip will go towards the community here.

Your time and skills can help us serve and love the people here. You get a vacation with a purpose. Everybody wins.

3. Consider spending less money somewhere else so you can give towards building the Village. I'm a missionary so you had to know this was coming. I ask for this confidently because I know the value of investing in eternal things rather than coffee and full closets. I also believe our money ultimately belongs to God and is only ours to use for a little while because God lets us.

4. Use our story as a catalyst to evaluate your life's purpose. If you have felt inspired or challenged in any way, pay attention to that. Ask yourself whether you are investing your time and energy in things that will outlast you. Maybe you needed our story as evidence that following Jesus can lead to great things. Maybe you needed our story to see what it can look like when God takes shattered lives and makes them whole. If so, keep the story going. Tell it to your friends over coffee or give them this book. The end of the best stories is only the beginning.

For more information on ACE, including our Green Life Village business plan, go to www.acexperience.org or visit our Facebook page. You can also reach us at 1-877-500-5768.

Teaching a group under the mango tree

Marla and Veazey, Marla's elder that commissioned her to Jamaica

Marla with Pastor Kermit Jones, former board member

Galina Breeze 2013

Typical day of youth who have dropped out of school

Marla's mentor and faithful friend (grandmother Verna Tracy)

A typical day in the field, Marla and Allen 2011

Marla and her men (Karl, Allen, and Horace) 2007

Marla and her men (Karl, Horace, and Allen) 2013

Dr. Steve Guy, medical missions director, heading to a medical clinic in 2004

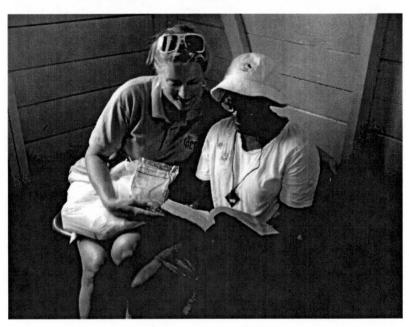

A prayer moment at Clinic

Dental team teaching Hampstead students about dental hygiene

Gary, fisherman and microbusiness recipient for
restoring his boat and rehulling his engine

Another microbusiness at Galina Breeze providing jerk
chicken to hotel patrons as well as anyone passing by

Green Life Farm Team (Coach and Mr. Myers)

Growing sustainability off the Green Life Farms

Dr. Luther Hughes teaching local farm about slow drip irrigation

Green Life Farm irrigation demonstration to students

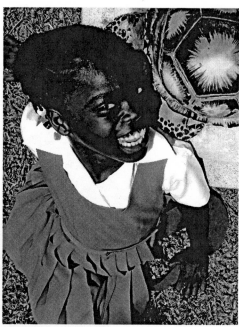

Tutoring our students sight words

A smile says it all after a field trip to Turtle Park

New uniforms for our sponsored student

Amber, full time child development coordinator with her children

A child sponsorship family. (Dian Burchell and children)

Mother of child sponsor student

Galina canning club

Building of the children's village

Children's Village model in the making

Red and Evyon, residents at the St. Mary Infirmary

Infirmary resident, Mr. Egbert eating Juice Patty

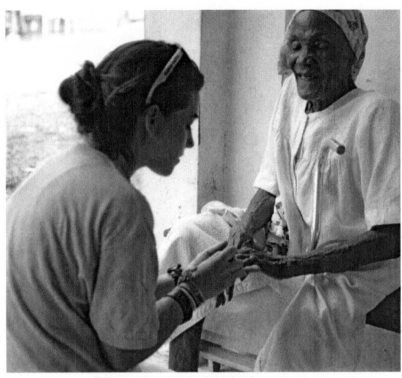

Volunteer assisting our infirmary residents

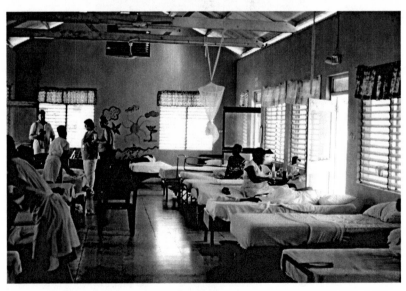

Inside of Infirmary

Thrift Sale - a great way to give but not give away

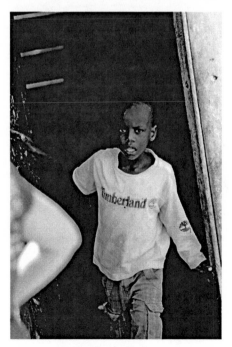

Thrift sale clothes

CPSIA information can be obtained at www.ICGtesting.com
Printed in the USA
BVOW05s2217120614

356215BV00017B/95/P

9 781622 451579